THE CHRISTIAN AND DRINKING
A BIBLICAL PERSPECTIVE ON
MODERATION AND ABSTINENCE

RANDY JAEGGLI

BOB JONES
UNIVERSITY PRESS
Greenville, South Carolina

Library of Congress Cataloging-in-Publication Data

Jaeggli, Randy, 1952–
    The Christian and drinking : a biblical perspective on moderation and absti-
nence / Randy Jaeggli.
        p. cm.
    Summary: "A study on the beverage use of alcohol"—Provided by publisher.
    Includes bibliographical references (p.   ).
    ISBN 978-1-59166-919-7 (perfect bound pbk. : alk. paper)
    1. Temperance (Virtue) 2. Moderation—Religious aspects—Christianity.
3. Drinking of alcoholic beverages. 4. Alcohol—Biblical teaching. I. Title.

    BV4647.T4J34 2008
    241'.681—dc22

                                                                    2008024789

**The Christian and Drinking: A Biblical Perspective on Moderation
and Abstinence**
Randy Jaeggli

Design by Rita Golden
Page layout by Michael Boone

© 2008 BJU Press
Greenville, South Carolina 29614
Bob Jones University Press is a division of BJU Press

Printed in the United States of America
All rights reserved

ISBN 978-1-59166-919-7

15   14   13   12   11   10   9   8   7   6   5   4   3   2   1

To Matt, Mike, and Mark—my three sons.
May they always be examples of the believer.

CONTENTS

PREFACE

Faithful Christians in every generation hunger for *Biblical Discernment for Difficult Issues*, the title of this book series authored by the faculty of Bob Jones University Seminary. The true disciple thirsts for a life that reflects Christ's love for others while striving to maintain loyalty to God's revealed Truth, the Scriptures. But as every mature Christian soon learns, demonstrating both God's compassion and God's holiness in this life is a balance that is never easy to strike.

Our propensity to wander from the right path is enough to alarm any honest follower of Christ. How quickly in our pursuit of holiness we do race into the darkness of a harsh, unforgiving condemnation of others who somehow lack the light we enjoy. And how tragically inclined we all are to slip, while on the narrow way, from the firm ground of genuine compassion into the mire of an unbiblical naiveté or an unwise sentimentality. Only by God's grace can the believer combine that loving compassion and that pursuit of a rigorous holiness into one life to bring the true "light of the knowledge of the glory of God in the face of Jesus Christ" to a needy church and a lost world.

The aim of this series is to provide help in finding this right, discerning balance in spiritual life without sacrificing one crucial emphasis in Scripture for another. While written in an easy-to-read style, these works attempt to combine mature, penetrating theological thought with thorough research. They aim to provide both a fact-intensive exposition of Scripture and a piercing application of it to real human experience. Hopefully those who read will find themselves making significant strides forward on the way to a renewed mind and a transformed life for the glory of Christ.

Stephen J. Hankins, Dean

Bob Jones University Seminary

INTRODUCTION

"So you've read our constitution and by-laws? Any questions?"

"No, Pastor, they're pretty clear."

"Doctrinal statement?"

"That too. We agree with it right down the line."

"And you've been baptized, so I don't see any obstacles to membership."

"I have just one more question, Pastor."

"Fire away."

"What's your church's position on alcohol?"

(Chuckle.) "As a disinfectant or as a beverage?"

"As a beverage."

"Well, the Bible pretty clearly forbids drunkenness, and we think the best way to avoid that is to just abstain from drinking altogether."

"So I can't have an occasional glass of wine if I join your church?"

"We covenant together to abstain, so, No."

"That's too bad, Pastor. I really like your church—the preaching, the teaching, the fellowship. I guess I'll just have to look somewhere else."

This conversation takes place more and more frequently. A good many Christians find themselves less and less convinced that social drinking violates the Scripture—and for some of them social drinking is an important part of their lifestyle. There's no ques-

1

tion that the culture of conservative Christianity has traditionally taught that drinking alcohol in any form is wrong, but as Christ clearly taught, the fact that "we've always done it that way" is a poor basis for doctrine or practice. Conservative Christians seek to believe and do what the Bible teaches—and more and more Christians, with good hearts and a desire to please God, are asking whether the Bible really teaches complete abstinence from alcoholic beverages of all kinds. That's a question that needs answering. What does the Bible, by direct statement, principle, and example, teach about drinking alcohol in moderation?

We should start by defining what we're talking about. There are many varieties of alcohol. Ingesting methanol in even small quantities can cause blindness and death. But add an extra carbon atom and two hydrogen atoms to methanol, and the product is ethanol, also known as ethyl alcohol. Ethanol is a natural by-product of the process of fermentation. When grapes are squeezed, the yeast that has been residing on the skins enters the juice, and the fermentation process begins. The yeast organisms live by utilizing the energy that is released when the sugar in the juice breaks down, and carbon dioxide and ethanol are waste products from the reaction. This process continues until the concentration of ethanol in the juice reaches a level that is toxic to the yeast—usually not more than about fourteen percent ethanol. All of the yeast die, and fermentation ceases.

When a person drinks an alcoholic beverage, the ethanol begins to affect his nervous system, and strange things can happen if he drinks enough. Normally reserved people, for example, can become outgoing and gregarious. I saw this phenomenon on more than one occasion when I worked as a process engineer for the paper industry. Meetings of the Technical Association of the Pulp and Paper Industry were thinly veiled excuses for excessive consumption of beer, wine, and distilled liquor. Because I never drank along with my colleagues, I used to find out all sorts of interesting information (whether I wanted to hear it or not) from intoxicated individuals who were suddenly garrulous and dead-level honest.

Unfortunately the effects of ethanol on the human nervous system are not always so amusingly benign. Ethanol reduces response times in important motor skills. If intoxicated people attempt to drive cars, the results are too often deadly. Sometimes drunks become aggressive instead of overly communicative. A student of mine who works as a sheriff's deputy told me that well over ninety percent of the domestic dispute calls he has handled have involved intoxication. He said that the level of personal danger he sensed in such situations was sometimes difficult to handle.

According to the US Centers for Disease Control, 61% of Americans drink occasionally; about one-third have consumed five or more drinks in a single day in the past year. In 2005, more than 21,000 deaths were caused directly by alcohol; that figure doesn't include accidents or homicides.[1] In 2002, roughly two-thirds of those who physically abused their spouse or boyfriend/girlfriend were under the influence of alcohol when they did so.[2]

In light of the destruction of property, physical injury, mental anguish, death, and serious medical problems that accompany excessive consumption of alcohol, Christians must examine the Scripture to establish personal standards of conduct in regard to the question of whether or not to partake of alcoholic beverages. Attitudes toward drinking have been changing in broader evangel-

---

[1]National Center for Health Statistics, *Health, United States, 2007*, Table 68, and *Deaths: Final Data for 2005*, National Vital Statistics Reports, vol. 56, no. 10; both cited in National Center for Health Statistics, *Faststats*, "Alcohol Use," http://www.cdc.gov/nchs/fastats/alcohol.htm.

[2]U.S. Department of Justice, Office of Justice Programs, Bureau of Justice Statistics, "Crime Characteristics," 2005, http://www.ojp.usdoj.gov/bjs/cvict_c.htm#alcohol.

icalism during the last fifty years. In contrast to the first half of the twentieth century, when most Bible-believing Americans held to a position of abstinence, attitudes toward drinking began to change in the 1960s. James Davison Hunter analyzed a survey of what students from nine evangelical liberal-arts colleges and seven seminaries believed concerning a wide range of theological and moral issues. The largest change in students' views concerning standards of moral conduct involved the issue of drinking alcoholic beverages. In 1951, 98% of students in these institutions agreed that it was always wrong to drink alcohol, but that percentage dropped to only 17% by 1982.[3] The percentage of those who reject the use of alcohol has probably fallen even further in the twenty-five years since the survey was done.

A number of Christians argue for total abstinence on the basis of the assertion that "wine" in the Bible was always unfermented when persons drank it appropriately. For example, William Patton's *Bible Wines or the Laws of Fermentation* is an older work that attempts to explain the seeming paradox between verses that commend wine as a blessing for God's people and other passages that warn of wine's dangerous qualities. Patton insists that wine is non-alcoholic grape juice in the former category of verses and alcoholic in the latter.[4] A more academic and modern attempt to prove the same premise is *The Biblical Approach to Alcohol*.[5] While all Christians can certainly appreciate the attempts that these works represent, one gets the impression that the authors started with an idea about what the Bible teaches and then made it teach what they wanted.

---

[3]James Davison Hunter, *Evangelicalism: the Coming Generation* (Chicago: The University of Chicago Press, 1987), 58–60.

[4]William Patton, *Bible Wines or the Laws of Fermentation* (Little Rock: The Challenge Press, n.d.), 11. This is a nineteenth-century work occasioned by the author's personal observation of displays of debauchery in New York City in 1820 (9–10).

[5]Stephen M. Reynolds, *The Biblical Approach to Alcohol* (Glenside, PA: L. L. Reynolds Foundation, 2003), 1–25.

As our survey of the biblical data will show, it is difficult to conclude that biblical wine was unfermented.

A fair evaluation of the way Scripture uses various Hebrew and Greek words for *wine* and *strong drink* demonstrates that they all refer to alcoholic beverages. People in biblical times sometimes drank in moderation, and other times they did not. The blessings or disaster they encountered depended on their moderation or their excessive consumption. (Of course this does not necessarily mean that moderate drinking is fine for today. As we shall see, there are many factors that play into that decision.) We must be careful not to extend our knowledge of microorganisms and pasteurization three thousand years into the past. Above all we must never come to the Bible with an idea of what we would like it to mean and force it to say what we think it should.

So what does the Bible say? And how are we to apply what it says to the question of alcoholic beverages today? As we shall see, a cavalier attitude toward even moderate consumption of alcohol is not warranted by Scripture.

1

OLD TESTAMENT TEACHING ON ALCOHOLIC BEVERAGES

The first step in evaluating the beverage use of alcohol is to examine what the Bible teaches explicitly about the subject. The Scripture is completely sufficient for a mature Christian life of service for God that is based on sound doctrine (2 Tim. 3:16–17). Our task is to make sure that we do a good job of interpreting the Scripture, lest we formulate our standards for Christian living on a faulty understanding of what God has actually revealed to us.[1]

Ancient people had neither the desire nor the ability to keep grape juice from fermenting. Because all natural beverages from fruit and grains would eventually ferment but were not distilled, none of them could have had an alcohol content of more than about fourteen percent.[2] Distillation can produce far higher ethanol content but was not discovered until the Middle Ages. Our discussion focuses on the words the Old Testament uses in referring to these fermented liquids.

---

[1] The discussion that follows unavoidably deals with some technical details of exegetical significance. The footnotes discuss matters that may be beyond the reader's level of linguistic comprehension. Some readers will wish to skip over details of Hebrew grammar and center more on what they can glean from the overall interpretive viewpoint.

[2] Non-fortified wines range from 8 to 14% ethanol. The percentage of sugar in the grape at the time of harvest (most wine grapes contain from 21 to 25% sugar) and the specific kind of yeast involved in fermentation determine the final percentage. Fermentation ceases at around 14%, no matter how high the sugar content of the grape juice, because that concentration of ethanol is lethal to the yeast. See Maynard A. Amerine, "Wine," in *Collier's Encyclopedia*, ed. Lauren S. Bahr (New York: P. F. Collier, 1996), 23:517–21.

Yayin[3]

The most common word in the Old Testament for alcoholic beverage is *yayin*, translated by the English word *wine*. This Hebrew word occurs 141 times.[4] We will examine representative uses in various categories of meaning.

The production of wine was a lot of work. Isaiah 5:1–7 describes God's relationship with Judah in the language of viticulture. First the Lord looked for a spot to plant His vineyard until He found the perfect "fruitful hill." He then dug up the soil, cleared away the rocks, and planted the best type of vine. He built a watchtower in the vineyard to protect it from human thieves or destructive animals. The last step was to hew a wine vat out of solid rock. According to A. C. Schultz, harvesters brought grapes in baskets and emptied them into the large upper section of the vat, where people would tread the grapes with their bare feet. The grape juice, or *must*, then flowed into a series of lower, deeper collection vats. Fermentation would begin almost immediately. After approximately a week of rapid fermentation and production of carbon-dioxide gas, the vintner would draw the wine from the vat into jars or wineskins, where the fermentation process would continue more slowly to completion. The wine would be ready for drinking in about two to four months.[5]

---

[3] יַיִן (pron. YĂ yĭn)

[4] For further study see W. Dommershausen, "יַיִן," in *Theological Dictionary of the Old Testament*, ed. G. Johannes Botterweck and Helmer Ringgren, trans. David E. Green (Grand Rapids: Eerdmans, 1990), 6:59–64; Eugene Carpenter, "יַיִן," in *New International Dictionary of Old Testament Theology and Exegesis*, ed. Willem A. VanGemeren (Grand Rapids: Zondervan, 1997), 2:439–41; and R. Laird Harris, "יַיִן," in *Theological Wordbook of the Old Testament*, ed. R. Laird Harris (Chicago: Moody, 1980), 2:375–76.

[5] A. C. Schultz, "Wine and Strong Drink," in *The Zondervan Pictorial Encyclopedia of the Bible*, ed. Merrill C. Tenney (Grand Rapids: Zondervan, 1976), 5:936–38.

Wine Identified as a Blessed Provision for Life

An essential part of biblical interpretation is to avoid reading our cultural setting back into the Old Testament. In our culture we have many options for non-alcoholic beverages from which to choose. Next to the regular faucet on my kitchen sink, for instance, is a smaller tap that dispenses water from my reverse osmosis filtration system. Before the water even enters the reverse osmosis filter, it goes through an activated charcoal pre-filter. Before it goes to the tap, the water passes through another charcoal finishing filter. One cannot imagine purer water anywhere on earth, except for distilled water. All I have to do is flip a lever, and I have all the safe hydration I need. Dying of thirst has never even crossed my mind.

The situation in the ancient world was much different. Although there were wells that were famous for supplying life-sustaining water (2 Sam. 23:15), many water sources were polluted by surface run-off bearing microorganisms that could produce serious illness. Since adequate hydration is essential for life, ancient people sought alternatives to tainted water.

One clue concerning the use of *yayin* as a necessary provision for sustaining life is its association in the Old Testament with items that were staples in a typical diet. When Abraham was returning from battle against the multinational confederacy that had taken Lot and the inhabitants of Sodom captive, he met the mysterious Melchizedek, priest of the Most High God. Melchizedek supplied Abraham with bread and wine (Gen. 14:18), just what the patriarch required to replenish his body's needs. The author of Judges tells us that the Levite and his concubine had all their needs met when they arrived in Gibeah: straw and fodder for the donkeys, and bread and wine for themselves (Judg. 19:19). When Abigail brought David the provisions he had requested from her husband, the list of items included wine (1 Sam. 25:18). As David fled from Jerusalem during the rebellion led by his son Absalom, Ziba met the king with life-sustaining provisions, including bread, raisins, summer fruits, and wine (2 Sam. 16:1). Ziba specifically said that the wine was for anyone who might be "faint in the wilderness" (v. 2).

Psalm 104:10–17 is perhaps the most striking passage presenting wine as a blessing from God for the satisfying of daily needs. God provides flowing springs of water for every wild animal of the field and bird of the heavens (vv. 10–12). The rain He sends causes grass to grow for cattle and food for man (vv. 13–14). The psalmist includes with these gifts in verse 15, "wine that maketh glad the heart of man, and oil to make his face to shine, and bread which strengtheneth man's heart." Alexander gives a possible alternate translation of the verse: "And wine gladdens the heart of man—(so as) to make his face shine more than oil—and bread the heart of man sustains."[6] Regardless of which translation is better, it is certain that the psalmist includes wine in a passage that extols God for His work of sustaining life on planet Earth.

Psalm 104:15 causes the reader to ponder whether wine gladdens man's heart in the sense of the alcohol's production of a euphoric state of mind, or whether the gladness is a result of recognizing that God has graciously met man's need for sustenance. The form of the Hebrew verb, "to make something glad,"[7] occurs in other contexts where the heart of man is made glad. Solomon says in Proverbs 27:9, for instance, that ointment and perfume make the heart glad. Here a glad heart finds delight in substances that please one's

---

[6]Joseph Addison Alexander, *The Psalms: Translated and Explained* (rpt. ed., 1873; Grand Rapids: Baker, 1975), 423–24. Alexander's translation depends on the use of the *min* preposition as comparative. The NASB takes *min* as causal:

"And wine which makes man's heart glad,

So that he may make his face glisten with oil,

And food which sustains man's heart."

[7]The verb is the Piel of שמח (*samach*).

senses. Proverbs 15:30 says, "Light of eyes makes a heart glad" (a literal translation). The NIV translates this verse, "A cheerful look brings joy to the heart." People like to be around others who are pleasant. Sometimes a smile and genuinely amicable greeting can lift a person's spirits. Proverbs 12:25 states, "Anxiety in the heart of a man weighs it down, but a good word makes it glad" (NASB). There is nothing like good news to brighten one's outlook on life.

Perhaps the most interesting use of the verb "to make [something] glad" is found in Ecclesiastes 10:19. Here we find the elements of bread and wine, just as in Psalm 104:15. "For enjoyment one makes bread, and wine gladdens life, and money answers everything" (my literal translation). All three provisions a person needs in life—food, drink, and economic resources—enhance his sense of well-being and satisfaction. We may safely conclude, therefore, that Psalm 104:15 speaks of wine gladdening a person's heart in the sense of satisfying his personal needs and enhancing his enjoyment of life. Based on the clear meaning of similar contexts, the verse does *not* extol the alcoholic "high" a person would get from excessive consumption of wine.

The scriptural authors sometimes utilize this concept of wine as a satisfaction of life's basic needs in order to picture in metaphoric language the benefits that wisdom offers to those who come to God with receptive hearts. In Proverbs 9:2–12 Solomon personifies wisdom as someone who has set her[8] table with food and wine,

---

[8]Because the Hebrew word for *wisdom* is a feminine noun, the English versions uniformly translate any pronouns referring to it as feminine ("she" or "her"). The reader should not think, however, that Solomon is portraying wisdom as a female. There is no masculinity or femininity implied in the gender of an inanimate noun. For a fuller discussion, see Bruce K. Waltke and M. O'Connor, *An Introduction to Biblical Hebrew Syntax* (Winona Lake, IN: Eisenbrauns, 1990), 99–110. Since Hebrew requires agreement between the gender of a noun and any verb or pronoun associated with it, the English versions may cause the reader to adopt the mistaken notion that wisdom must be a woman.

the dietary items necessary for sustaining life. Notice that she has "mixed her wine" (v. 2). Waltke maintains that wisdom personified "added something like honey and/or herbs to make the wine more spicy, potent, and enjoyable, not that she diluted it with water." But then he notes the rabbinic view that dilution with water was indeed being described. Waltke also notes that the Septuagint translators rendered the verb "to mix" as "to mix in a bowl." This translation reflects the ancient Greek practice of diluting wine with water in a mixing bowl.[9] Keep this thought in mind, because we will return in chapter three to a discussion of the practice of diluting wine in the ancient world.

The prophet Isaiah built on the concept of wine as an essential commodity for physical life as he crafted a metaphor that pictured eternal life. In the language of a vendor selling his wares in the streets of Jerusalem, Isaiah cried out, "Ho, every one that thirsteth, come ye to the waters, and he that hath no money; come ye, buy, and eat; yea, come, buy wine and milk without money and without price" (Isa. 55:1). God is so gracious in salvation that He makes eternal life free to all who will receive it.[10] Just as milk and wine sustain physical life, so the salvation that God offers satisfies man's soul and gladdens his heart forever.

The blessing of wine consumption as a necessary provision for life always depended on the moderation of its use. Solomon admonished

---

[9]Bruce K. Waltke, *The Book of Proverbs: Chapters 1–15*, in The New International Commentary on the Old Testament, ed. R. K. Harrison and Robert L. Hubbard, Jr. (Grand Rapids: Eerdmans, 2004), 434. In his discussion about wine, Harris notes, "To avoid the sin of drunkenness, mingling of wine with water was practiced. This dilution was specified by the Rabbis in NT times for the wine then customary at Passover" (Harris, 376).

[10]J. Alec Motyer correctly notes, "Yet alongside this emphasis on freeness, the verb *buy* is repeated. The thought of purchase is not set aside; this is no soup-kitchen, even if the clients are beggars. There is a purchase and a price, though not theirs to pay. They bring their poverty to a transaction already completed. Contextually, this is another allusion to the work of the Servant." *The Prophecy of Isaiah: An Introduction and Commentary* (Downers Grove, IL: InterVarsity, 1993), 453.

his sons, "Be not among winebibbers; among riotous eaters of flesh: For the drunkard and the glutton shall come to poverty: and drowsiness shall clothe a man with rags" (Prov. 23:20–21). The word *winebibbers* translates a Hebrew participle from a verb meaning "to carouse," or "to drink hard."[11] The participle conveys the idea of habitual, heavy drinking. Notice the way Solomon associates excessive drinking of wine with gluttony as producing equally disastrous consequences in a person's life. Just as the glutton does not know when to push away from the table, so the alcoholic refuses to put his wine goblet down and walk away from his drink. The key to whether wine consumption is a blessing or a curse lies in the heart attitude of the person who drinks.[12] Solomon declares, "He that loveth pleasure shall be a poor man: he that loveth wine and oil shall not be rich" (Prov. 21:17). Wine and oil were blessings from God, and He intended His people to enjoy these gifts without fixing their love on them.

Wine Is Easily Abused

Unfortunately anything good can be abused. Consider, for instance, the recreational activities many people in our society enjoy. Recreation provides good exercise and a release from the stress many of us experience. But hobbies, sports, and avid interests can sometimes get out of control in a person's life. What started out as a good thing becomes an obsession, consuming inordinate amounts of financial resources, time, and mental planning. People in biblical times were prone to take God's gift of wine and abuse

---

[11]See William L. Holladay, *A Concise Hebrew and Aramaic Lexicon of the Old Testament* (Grand Rapids: Eerdmans, 1971), s.v. סבא, 251.

[12]The heart attitude of the believer towards money is another example of this principle that something good can produce harm if we are not careful. The Christian ought to view money dispassionately as a tool to meet his needs and the needs of others. Danger arises, however, when a person loves money. Indeed, "the love of money is the root of all evil: which while some coveted after, they have erred from the faith, and pierced themselves through with many sorrows" (1 Tim. 6:10).

it. The biblical authors have much to say about the sin of excessive consumption of wine.

The first instance in Scripture of the sin of alcohol abuse occurs in the account of Noah. At a time when "the wickedness of man was great in the earth" (Gen. 6:5), "Noah found grace in the eyes of the Lord" (v. 8). Noah obeyed the Lord, labored faithfully in the construction of the ark, and fulfilled God's will. Through his efforts God saved the world from destruction. After Noah and his family disembarked from their floating sanctuary and God instituted a covenant with them, however, Moses records next that Noah planted a vineyard, drank from the wine he produced, and became drunk (Gen. 9:20–21). In his drunken state he displayed a loss of propriety by lying naked in his tent. His sin became the occasion for Ham's sin, which resulted in the curse on Canaan.[13] The reader of the Genesis narrative is absolutely astounded! After all that God did in showing grace to Noah, this godly man could not control his intake of wine. Because this sin felled such a godly man, every believer should take warning. Noah's sin also affected succeeding generations, just as alcohol abuse commonly does today.

Ingesting excessive amounts of wine can suspend a person's sense of morality to the point where he will commit incest. After the deliverance of Lot from the destruction of Sodom and Gomorrah, his two daughters on sequential nights got their father drunk with wine and engaged in incestuous relations with him (Gen. 19:31–35). After both of these incestuous events, Lot was so inebriated that in

---

[13]It is beyond the scope of our discussion to delve into what the nature of Ham's sin was, or why Ham was cursed in Canaan. For an excellent discussion of Ham's sin, see Victor P. Hamilton, *The Book of Genesis: Chapters 1–17*, in The New International Commentary on the Old Testament, ed. R. K. Harrison and Robert L. Hubbard, Jr. (Grand Rapids: Eerdmans, 1990), 322–23. Geerhardus Vos maintains that Ham was cursed in Canaan "because he had sinned against his father, and he was punished in that particular son, because Canaan most strongly reproduced Ham's sensual character." *Biblical Theology: Old and New Testaments* (Grand Rapids: Eerdmans, 1948), 57.

neither case did he have any knowledge of when his daughter "lay down, nor when she arose" (vv. 33, 35). Just as in the narrative about Noah, we know that Lot was a righteous man. Abraham had received God's promise that He would not destroy Sodom and Gomorrah if ten righteous individuals lived there. Abraham successfully argued, and the Lord did not rebut his assertion, that it would be unjust for the Lord to sweep the righteous away with the wicked in judgment (Gen. 18:23–32). The angels' action of dragging Lot out of Sodom before the judgment could fall proves his righteous standing before God. Lot had vexed his righteous soul with the sin of Sodom (2 Pet. 2:8), but alcohol snared him.

Excessive wine consumption can also anesthetize a person to the extent that he is oblivious to imminent danger. In 2 Samuel 13 we encounter one of the saddest narratives in the Bible: David's son Amnon raped his half-sister Tamar. When Tamar told Absalom what had happened, he seemed to downplay the matter. But because Tamar was his full sister, Absalom's hatred of Amnon burned within his heart for two years. Finally Absalom saw his chance for revenge. He persuaded David to send Amnon and all the king's sons to a sheep-shearing event. Absalom carefully instructed his servants, "Mark ye now when Amnon's heart is merry with wine,[14] and when I say unto you, Smite Amnon; then kill him" (2 Sam. 13:28). The plan worked perfectly. Amnon was so drunk that he was virtually defenseless. So it happens today that inebriated people drive their cars and are oblivious to the mortal danger that faces them down the road.

Addiction to alcohol also destroys wisdom. Proverbs 20:1 says, "Wine is a mocker, strong drink is raging; and whosoever is deceived thereby

---

[14]The phrase "when a heart is merry" is the Hebrew כְּטוֹב לֵב. The only other occurrence of the construction is in Esther 1:10, describing the inebriated state of King Ahasuerus.

is not wise." The "mocker" (sometimes translated "scorner" by the KJV) is the most hopeless category of fool in the book of Proverbs. If a person tries to correct a mocker, all he will get is dishonor and hatred (Prov. 9:7–8). The mocker is very proud (21:24), and the only thing to do with him is to apply corporal discipline (19:25; 21:11) or banish him (22:10). Waltke correctly notes that wine is personified in 20:1 in order to warn people that this intoxicant has the potential to produce in them the very characteristics of the mocker that Solomon delineates throughout the book of Proverbs. "The drunkard lacks consciousness and self-control, and in dissolute madness breaks the bounds of sanctity, morality, and propriety."[15] The phrase "whosoever is deceived thereby" is literally "everyone who is staggering in it."[16] This is clearly a description of a person who is highly inebriated. Because wisdom is the most precious characteristic a person can possess (Prov. 8:11), anything that causes the loss of wisdom should be viewed as horrifically dangerous.

Solomon exposed the dangers of wine by placing a warning about the attractiveness of the beverage immediately after a description of an adulterous woman or a prostitute (Prov. 23:27–35). These immoral women are a "deep ditch" or a "narrow pit" (v. 27). They lie in wait for prey, just as a predatory animal does (v. 28). Earlier in the book Solomon warned his sons that the immoral woman can make herself and her sin seem extremely attractive. "For the lips of a strange woman drop as an honeycomb, and her mouth is smoother than oil" (5:3). Here Solomon uses "lips" and "mouth"

---

[15]Bruce K. Waltke, *The Book of Proverbs: Chapters 15–31*, in The New International Commentary on the Old Testament, ed. R. K. Harrison and Robert L. Hubbard, Jr. (Grand Rapids: Eerdmans, 2005), 126. Waltke also has an extended discussion of the way Scripture sometimes describes wine in a favorable way and notes that Proverbs 20:1 "protects itself against contradicting this favorable side of wine and beer *by restricting it to the inebriated*" (127, emphasis added).

[16]The word translated "who is staggering" is a Qal active participle from שׁגה. For the meaning "stagger, be unable to walk straight," see Holladay, 361.

by metonymy to represent speech. The immoral woman will say anything in order to ensnare her prey. Her speech is sexy and seductive, geared to focus a man's thoughts on how desirable she is—not on her immorality. Solomon also commanded his sons not to allow the immoral woman to captivate them with her beauty (6:25). Then Solomon recounted an experience of seeing an act of seduction unfolding before his very eyes (7:6–27). The immoral woman did everything she could think of to make adultery look attractive. She told her intended victim, "I have decked my bed with coverings of tapestry, with carved works, with fine linen of Egypt. I have perfumed my bed with myrrh, aloes, and cinnamon" (vv. 16–17).

Solomon intended the full impact of his teaching about the immoral woman's attractiveness to inform his sons' understanding about the dangerous, pleasant appearance of wine. He declared, "Look not thou upon the wine when it is red, when it giveth his colour in the cup, when it moveth itself aright" (Prov. 23:31). By centering their attention on the attractiveness of the wine, they might fall into the same sort of visually oriented trap the immoral woman sets up. The first part of verse 23 says, "You should not observe wine when it is red" (my translation). The verb that I have translated "observe" is ראה (ra'ah), normally glossed "to see." This verb occurs 1,303 times in the Old Testament and often conveys much more than a simple look at something.[17] The action Solomon is forbidding his sons is a careful observation that leads to sensual enjoyment. In Genesis 8:8 Noah sent out a dove *to see* whether the water had abated. His careful observation of the various activities of the dove caused him ultimately *to know* that he could exit the ark (v. 11). Likewise when the Queen of Sheba came to visit

---

[17]See the very thorough article by H. F. Fuhs, "רָאָה," in *Theological Dictionary of the Old Testament*, ed. G. Johannes Botterweck, Helmer Ringgren, and Heinz-Josef Fabry (Grand Rapids: Eerdmans, 2004), 13:208–42.

Solomon, her purpose was *to see* his wisdom. Her careful observation left her astounded (1 Kings 10:4–7). Sometimes the verb *to see* means to experience the enjoyment of something. In Isaiah 44:16, for instance, the foolish idolater, who has used half a log to make a wooden idol and the other half to make a fire, says, "Aha, I am warm, I have seen the fire." So when Solomon forbids his sons to "look" at wine, his injunction involves a longing gaze that regards enjoyment of the wine as a sensual experience.[18]

The modern equivalent would involve the typical presentation of wine in a fancy restaurant by a sommelier. This waiter carefully pours wine into a special glass and hands it to the patron who picked it from the menu. The patron then sniffs the bouquet, swirls the beverage in the glass, holds it up to the light, and takes a small taste. It is quite a production. The patron must be pleased with the wine's fragrance, color, overall appearance, and taste. He wants the total sensual experience an expensive wine can offer. This sort of fixation on the experience of drinking wine is exactly what Proverbs 23:31 forbids. Bruce Waltke correctly observes, "At the semantic center of the saying is the command not to yield to wine's temptation. Devastating consequences lampooning addiction surround it."[19]

Just as horrible consequences befall the foolish man who succumbs to the attractiveness of the immoral woman, so disaster comes on the man who is seduced by wine. Solomon asks his sons, "Who hath woe? Who hath sorrow? Who hath contentions? Who hath babbling? Who hath wounds without cause? Who hath redness of eyes?" (Prov. 23:29). The answer can be stated quite succinctly: "They that tarry long at the wine; they that go to seek mixed

---

[18]Some might object that we are often encouraged to observe and appreciate beautiful things and to exercise our senses to appreciate what God has made. Yet this passage seems to place such an extended appreciation of wine outside the bounds of appropriateness, because of the danger inherent in that activity.

[19]Waltke, *The Book of Proverbs: Chapters 15–31*, 262.

wine"[20] (v. 30). Those who allow themselves to become addicted to wine find that it bites like a snake and stings like a viper (v. 32). I like to spend time in the woods, especially during hunting season in the fall. I know there are copperheads residing somewhere in the fields and forests where I walk, and I sincerely hope I never get bitten by one. If I happened to see one, there is no predicting how fast I could move away from it. Solomon viewed addiction to wine this way—as a dangerous snake to avoid with all one's energy. Verse 33 warns that drunks can see some strange things[21] and speak things they will regret when sober. Changing to a nautical setting, Solomon warns that a drunk is like a person that "lieth down in the midst of the sea, or as he that lieth upon the top of a mast" (v. 34). In his drunken state he is so insensitive that he doesn't even know when someone strikes him. He is so addicted that immediately upon the dawning of a new day he seeks another drink (v. 35).

Wine Is a Metaphor of God's Judgment

Because addiction to wine has such deleterious personal consequences, it is an appropriate metaphor of God's judgment on sin. The Psalmist, for example, states concerning God's dealings with His people, "Thou hast shown thy people hard things: thou hast made us to drink the wine of astonishment" (Ps. 60:3 [Heb. v. 5]). The word translated "astonishment" occurs in the Old Testament only here and in Isaiah 51:17, 22. It refers to the staggering motion

---

[20]The term "mixed wine" is מִמְסָךְ. This noun occurs only here and in Isa. 65:11. The noun is related to the verb מָסַךְ used in Prov. 9:2. Wilma A. Bailey maintains that the noun refers to a mixing bowl in which wine and honey or spices would be combined. She does not discuss the possibility of dilution with water. "מסך," in *New International Dictionary of Old Testament Theology & Exegesis*, ed. Willem A. VanGemeren (Grand Rapids: Zondervan: 1997), 2:999–1000.

[21]The KJV translates the Hebrew as "strange women," but the feminine plural noun זָרוֹת probably means "strange, surprising things." See Holladay, 9.

of a drunk as he attempts to walk.[22] God's judgment has severe effects and leaves His people reeling from the anger their sin deserves.

Psalm 75:8 (Heb. v. 9) says, "For a cup is in the hand of the Lord, and the wine foams; It is well mixed, and He pours out of this; Surely all the wicked of the earth must drain and drink down its dregs" (NASB). The universality of this verse ("all the wicked of the earth") reminds the reader of the bowls of God's wrath poured out on the inhabitants of earth in the days of the Great Tribulation.[23] Revelation 16:19 announces, "And the great city was divided into three parts, and the cities of the nations fell: and great Babylon came in remembrance before God, to give unto her the cup of the wine of the fierceness of his wrath." There is a certain irony in the picture of God judging men by forcing them to drink wine right to the bottom of the vessel. Men have used wine in excess as part of their rebellion against Him. Now God will give them more "wine" than they care for, as they are filled to capacity with His outpoured wrath.

The Old Testament prophets spoke often against alcohol abuse in their culture. It is no wonder, therefore, that the consequences of excessive consumption of wine should picture God's judgment on sin. For instance, God demonstrates through the object lesson of Jeremiah's linen waistband that God had rejected His completely ruined nation. As a metaphor of the judgment that was fast approaching, the Lord told Jeremiah to proclaim, "Thus saith the Lord God of Israel, Every bottle shall be filled with wine" (Jer. 13:12).[24]

---

[22]See Holladay, s.v. "תַּרְעֵלָה," 395.

[23]See Willem A. VanGemeren, "Psalms," in *The Expositor's Bible Commentary*, ed. Frank E. Gaebelein (Grand Rapids: Zondervan, 1991), 5:493.

[24]F. B. Huey suggests that this was actually a well-known proverb in Judah. "The saying may have originated as a raucous cry at a drunken feast, but it probably had become a confident expression that God would continue to prosper the people. If so, Jeremiah turned it into a promise of certain judgment. . . . 'Drunkenness' here is a figure to describe the helplessness of the people to defend themselves from the enemy's

The thought of these storage jars[25] being full to capacity with wine was to remind the people that God was about to fill them with drunkenness and destruction (v. 13). The Lord promised that He would "dash them one against another, even the fathers and the sons together" (v. 14). Instead of picturing God's blessing and provision for His people, abundant wine signaled the approaching disaster of the Babylonian onslaught. Just as drunkenness produces disorientation, insensibility, and inability to recognize danger, so God's people were unaware of impending destruction.

Wine Is Sometimes to Be Avoided Completely

Due to the possible abuse of wine and its well-established use as a metaphor of coming judgment, God instructed His people that there were specific situations demanding total abstinence from the fruit of the vine. The earliest and most famous of these injunctions against wine involved the vow of the Nazirite. This was an entirely voluntary act that involved consecration of one's life totally to the Lord. The Nazirite was to abstain from any form of fermented beverage, even from non-alcoholic vinegar.[26] He could not drink freshly squeezed grape juice[27] or eat grapes or dried raisins (Num. 6:3). The vow precluded him from shaving his hair or beard and from contact with any dead body—even the corpse of one of his close relatives (vv. 5–7).

---

attack." *Jeremiah, Lamentations*, vol. 16 in *The New American Commentary*, ed. E. Roy Clendenen (Nashville: Broadman, 1993), 145.

[25]The Hebrew word נֵבֶל refers not to "bottles" (KJV) or "wineskins" (NIV), but to storage jars (Huey, 145).

[26]Fermentation is an anaerobic process involving yeast. The production of vinegar (acetic acid) is an aerobic process involving bacteria. (Acetic acid is simply a more highly oxidized product derived from ethanol.) Because vinegar came from a fermented source, it was likewise a banned substance for the Nazirite.

[27]The Hebrew word is מִשְׁרָה, a *hapax legomenon*. Holladay defines it as grape juice or grape extract (s.v. "מִשְׁרָה," 222).

The reason for a Nazirite's separation from anything associated with grapes is not explicitly clear. Freedom from the possibility of intoxication could not be the complete explanation for the avoidance of any grape product; raisins don't cause drunkenness. Perhaps J. Barton Payne captured the intent of the prohibition when he stated that grapes "stood as a symbol for all the temptations of the settled life in Canaan."[28] Payne's view finds support in the account of the twelve spies who brought back to the Israelites a report of what Canaan was like. Moses was careful to record that two spies carried a cluster of grapes from Canaan between them on a pole, presumably because the size and weight of the cluster precluded one man from being able to transport it (Num. 13:23–27). Here was proof that the land God had promised to give His people was remarkably fruitful. Along with the blessing, however, came the temptation of focusing more on the gift of the land than on the Giver of the gift. Nothing has the capacity for turning men's hearts away from God faster than prosperity. The Nazirite vow was the Lord's way of drawing His people's attention back to Him. The Nazirite stood out from the crowd by voluntarily abstaining from the enjoyments to which he was otherwise entitled, simply because he loved God and wanted to be separated exclusively for service to Him. Other Israelites who witnessed the sacrifice of the Nazirite would find unspoken exhortation to make sure that the prosperity of a settled life in Canaan had not robbed them of their devotion to the Lord.

In Jeremiah 35:1–18 we find another account of people who voluntarily refused to drink wine. According to Huey, the Rechabites were descended from a semi-nomadic group of Kenites. The Scripture first mentions them in relation to Israel's exodus from Egypt (mid-fifteenth century BC). About 250 years before Jeremiah's

---

[28]See "Nazirite, Nazarite," in *The Zondervan Pictorial Encyclopedia of the Bible*, ed. Merrill C. Tenney (Grand Rapids: Zondervan, 1976), 4:392.

day, a Rechabite named Jonadab had instructed his descendants never to build houses, plant vineyards, or drink wine.[29] The Lord instructed Jeremiah to bring these Rechabites into the temple, set bowls of wine and drinking cups before them, and command them to drink (Jer. 35:1–5). They refused to drink, solely because they were loyal to what Jonadab had instructed them 250 years previously (v. 6). The Lord used this occasion to draw the attention of His people to their disloyalty to the Mosaic covenant. Even though God had repeatedly sent His prophets to rebuke the people, those who should have obeyed God ignored His messengers' warning of imminent judgment. If the Rechabites could obey the injunctions of a human ancestor, then surely the inhabitants of Judah could be expected to obey the Sovereign over all.

The reader immediately wonders why Jonadab would have insisted that his descendants shun wine and city living. "Perhaps Jonadab became repulsed and disillusioned by the corruption and immorality he saw in city life and determined to separate himself and his family from its corrupting influences."[30] Whatever the reason, God rewarded them for faithfulness to their ancestor by promising that there would never fail to be a faithful Rechabite serving the Lord (Jer. 35:18–19). About 150 years after Jeremiah's day, God's blessing was still in effect (Neh. 3:14).

This narrative of the Rechabites demands application to our day. I grew up in a home where distilled liquor, beer, and wine were present. My parents drank, but they disdained drunkenness and always partook in moderation. After they trusted in Christ for salvation, however, the alcohol disappeared from our home. They never made an explicit point about why they got rid of it, but I inferred from the removal that they no longer approved of the use of alcohol.

[29]Huey, 312–13.
[30]Ibid., 315.

Some Christian parents take a much stronger stand. They explicitly teach their children that drinking alcoholic beverages is wrong. They warn of the potentially disastrous consequences of alcohol abuse. They point out that today we have many sources of safe, non-alcoholic hydration. They maintain that drinking in the ancient world is not equivalent to partaking of alcohol today. They insist that a consistent Christian testimony demands abstinence as the only proper manifestation of separation from the world system that makes drinking the test of peer acceptance. If a person rejects this sort of parental instruction, he turns his back on the principle that Jeremiah 35:1–18 should drive home to the hearts of believers: we must honor our parents.[31] Jonadab's offspring understood the association between obeying their ancestor's commands and honoring him. They were motivated to obey by trusting Jonadab's promise that they might "live many days in the land" where they sojourned (v. 7). This promise is quite similar to the command of the Decalogue, "Honor thy father and thy mother: that *thy days may be long upon the land* which the Lord thy God giveth thee" (Exod. 20:12, emphasis added). A Christian who breaks his parents' hearts by engaging in behavior they have strongly warned against has dishonored them.

The Bible makes the consumption of wine wrong for certain people at various times in their lives. In Proverbs 31:4–5 we find, for instance, that kings are to avoid wine because they might drink and pervert the justice due their subjects. Wine not only slows down physical response times but also blunts powers of reasoning. It is one thing for a person in a rural setting to be drunk at home where he has minimal effect on other people, but an entirely different

---

[31]Of course Christ Himself condemned those who followed "the traditions of the elders" in ways that opposed the greater commandments of God (e.g., Matt. 15:3; 23:23; Mark 7:8); honoring one's parents has its limits, and continuing in a parent's misguided practice has no merit and may be sinful. By contrast, then, God's rewarding the Rechabites' faithfulness to Jonadab's commandment seems to place His stamp of approval on it.

matter for a person with significant influence over other people to do anything that even slightly impairs his judgment.

Priests were also prohibited from drinking wine when they came into the tabernacle to perform their priestly duties (Lev. 10:9). The Lord was so emphatic about this injunction that He warned Aaron and his sons that the penalty for disobedience was death. Since this legislation immediately follows the account of Nadab and Abihu's act of offering "strange fire" before the Lord (10:13), R. Laird Harris notes that "there is more than a hint that Nadab and Abihu profaned the Lord's house because they were drunk."[32] The sacrificial system was complicated and required the full mental capacities of the priests. It is unwise for someone who represents the holy God of heaven to do anything purposely that reduces his ability to reason and carry out a detailed course of action.

TIROSH[33]

Yayin is not the only word the Old Testament uses in referring to alcoholic beverages. The word *tirosh* occurs much less frequently—only 38 times. The KJV translates it using three different concepts in English: *wine, new wine,* or *sweet wine.* Sometimes the word can refer to grape juice still in the cluster of grapes (Isa. 65:8). This would obviously be completely unfermented. Most often *tirosh* is the freshly squeezed juice from the grape that flows into a wine vat (e.g. Prov. 3:10). The word appears in most of its uses along with other agricultural products, such as grain and olive oil, and these items are viewed as blessings that Yahweh pours out on those who are obedient to His covenant. The book of Deuteronomy alone contains seven such references to *tirosh* as a blessing, one of which threatens the loss of agricultural provision if God's people persist

---

[32]R. Laird Harris, "Leviticus," in *The Expositor's Bible Commentary,* ed. Frank E. Gaebelein (Grand Rapids: Zondervan, 1990), 2:567.

[33] תִּירוֹשׁ (pron. TĒ rōsh)

in disobedience to His Word (Deut. 28:51). Because the book of Deuteronomy was Moses' last address to Israel before the nation entered Canaan to take the land God had promised to His people, Moses was careful to fortify God's people against the idolatrous viewpoint of the Canaanites. These wicked idolaters thought their worship of Baal, the god of fertility, ensured agricultural abundance for them. The Lord wanted to make sure the Israelites understood that Yahweh alone controls crop productivity. Consequently the Mosaic law specified that new wine was an essential component of the tithe of the firstfruits of the harvest in thanks for what Yahweh had given to His people (Deut. 12:17–18).

Although *tirosh* did not contain as much alcohol as fully fermented wine, it did have sufficient ethanol to cause drunkenness if a person consumed enough of it. Because grape juice starts fermenting almost immediately after it flows into the vat, even *tirosh* could be abused.[34] The prophet Hosea warned God's people that "whoredom and wine and new wine [*tirosh*] take away the heart" (4:11). The translation "take away the heart" is literal and idiomatic for "cause loss of understanding." Hosea makes the assertion that idolatry is spiritual adultery and causes a loss of cognitive ability just as surely as alcoholic beverages do.[35]

'ASIS[36]

Another word for freshly squeezed juice is *'asis*. This word occurs only five times in the Old Testament and is translated *juice, new wine,* or

---

[34]"Indeed to drink non-fermented juice was probably possible only briefly, in season, just as grapes were being tread [*sic*], because fermentation occurred quickly in Israel's warm climate." Jack M. Sasson, "The Blood of Grapes: Viticulture and Intoxication in the Hebrew Bible," in *Drinking in Ancient Societies: History and Culture of Drinks in the Ancient Near East*, ed. Lucio Milano (Padova, Italy: Sargon srl, 1994), 401.

[35]See Thomas Edward McComiskey, "Hosea," in *The Minor Prophets: An Exegetical and Expository Commentary*, ed. Thomas Edward McComiskey (Grand Rapids: Baker Academic, 1992), 1:66.

[36]עָסִיס (pron. ngah SĒS)

sweet wine by the KJV. Just as with the case of *tirosh*, *'asis* could produce drunkenness if a person consumed large enough quantities.[37] The prophet Isaiah declared that the time is coming when Yahweh will rescue His people from their oppressors (Isa. 49:24–25). At that time "they shall be drunken with their own blood, as with sweet wine [*'asis*]: and all flesh shall know that I the Lord am thy Saviour and thy Redeemer, the mighty One of Jacob" (v. 26).

SHEKAR[38]

The final word we will examine in the class of alcoholic beverages is *shekar*, translated by the KJV as *strong drink* in all but one of its 23 occurrences (Num. 28:7 is the exception). The Hebrew verb to which it is related means "to be drunk." Because of this semantic connection, P. P. Jenson postulates that originally *shekar* was a general word for the entire semantic range of alcoholic beverages. Then as wine made from grapes became popular in Palestine, *shekar* became a term that referred to any alcoholic drink made from something other than grapes.[39] Marvin A. Powell notes that beer made from the fermentation of grains is well attested in the Ancient Near East as far back as early Sumerian culture. He also questions whether the term *beer* may be completely accurate. It is possible that the favorite Babylonian beverage was more like *kvass*, a brew that has only about 0.5% ethanol (about one-tenth the content of modern beer) and has long been popular in Eastern Europe and Russia.[40] Our modern notions about certain beverages may not accurately describe what ancient people drank.

---

[37]See Eugene Carpenter, "עָסִיס," in *New International Dictionary of the Old Testament*, ed. Willem A. VanGemeren (Grand Rapids: Zondervan, 1997), 3:470.

[38]שֵׁכָר (pron. SHAY kar)

[39]P. P. Jenson, "שכר," in *New International Dictionary of Old Testament Theology and Exegesis*, ed. Willem A. VanGemeren (Grand Rapids: Zondervan, 1997), 4:113.

[40]Marvin A. Powell, "Metron Ariston: Measure as a Tool for Studying Beer in Ancient Mesopotamia," in *Drinking in Ancient Societies*, 91.

The term *shekar* appears in the majority of its uses paired with the word *wine*. We have already seen that priests were forbidden to drink wine before they came into the tabernacle to perform their duties. They were also prohibited from drinking *shekar* (Lev. 10:9). A Nazirite couldn't drink *shekar* any more than he could consume wine (Num. 6:3). The Lord asserted that Israel drank no *shekar* or wine all their years spent wandering in the wilderness (Deut. 29:6). So what is true of wine is also true of *shekar*. When Eli accused Hannah of being drunk, she asserted that she had consumed neither *shekar* nor wine (1 Sam. 1:15). We can safely conclude, therefore, that the two words together describe the spectrum of alcoholic beverages available to people in biblical times.

CONCLUSION

We have seen that God intended His people to view alcoholic beverages as a blessing from His hand, just as they appreciated all agricultural products from the land He had given. At a time in history when potable water was not always readily available, alcoholic beverages provided a safe means of hydration—a necessity for life. We have also seen from Proverbs 9:2 that ancient Israelites most likely did exactly what later Jews most certainly did: they mixed their wine with water just before drinking it.[41] The term the KJV renders *strong drink* may also have had a much lower alcohol content than

---

[41]Some sources maintain, on the basis of Isaiah 1:22, that ancient Israelites did not mix water with their wine. Schultz, for example, states with certainty that "in the OT period, wine was used at full strength because diluting it with water was considered undesirable. Wine diluted with water became symbolical of spiritual adulteration (Isa. 1:22)" (935). Schultz fails to notice, however, that Isa. 1:22 uses a word for wine (סבא) that occurs only three times in the Old Testament. Holladay suggests that it might be a word for beer (251). In Isa. 56:12 the related verb סבא occurs with the noun *strong drink* and is differentiated from the phrase "I will fetch wine" earlier in the verse. We can conclude that סבא is an alcoholic beverage different from wine. I imagine that watered-down beer would be rather uninviting, especially if the water came from some unknown source of contamination.

modern beer. It is a serious mistake for today's believer to assume that modern alcoholic beverages are equivalent to ancient drinks.

Even if ancient beverages had lower alcohol content, however, the possibility of drunkenness was a real danger if a person drank heavily enough. Wine was a blessing only if consumed moderately. The Old Testament contains serious warnings against intemperance. Drunkenness can suspend moral judgment, leading to sin that can affect even future generations. Excessive consumption of alcohol can destroy a person's awareness of danger and so cloud mental reasoning that obedience to God's Word becomes impossible. Alcoholic beverages are a potential trap, full of poisonous snakes and as alluring as a crafty prostitute.

Alcoholic beverages picture the effects of God's judgment. The picture of a drunk staggering as he tries to walk serves as a metaphor for the massive disorientation, incapacitation, and imminent danger people face as God pours out His wrath on man's sin. Just as a drunk has far too much to drink, so sinners will drain the cup of God's fury down to the very dregs. Someday the universal effects of God's judgment will cause the entire earth to "reel to and fro like a drunkard" (Isa. 24:20).

As an opposite metaphor to judgment, abstinence from alcohol pictures complete devotion to Yahweh. The life of the Nazirite made him an oddity during the time of his vow. Everywhere he went, his long hair and untrimmed beard were a sign for everyone to see that this person had voluntarily kept himself from things other people could enjoy. A king who aspired to fairness and equity distanced himself from alcohol. The priest who desired to show his people the way of approach to their holy God never drank alcoholic beverages while serving the Lord.

2

NEW TESTAMENT TEACHING ON ALCOHOLIC BEVERAGES

The vocabulary of alcoholic beverages in the New Testament is much less varied and developed than in the Old Testament. The main word for wine in the New Testament is *oinos*, corresponding to the Old Testament word *yayin*. There is also one occurrence of the Greek word *gleukos*, wine that has not completely fermented.

OINOS[1]

The Greek word *oinos* occurs 34 times in the New Testament. Its potential for producing intoxication is apparent in Paul's command, "And be not drunk with wine, wherein is excess, but be filled with the Spirit" (Eph. 5:18). The verb *methuskō* ("to be drunk") is always passive in form in the New Testament but conveys a condition that one has brought upon himself.[2] Paul does not forbid drinking wine, only drinking to excess. In addition to commanding avoidance of drunkenness, Paul states the positive command "but be filled with the Spirit." The idea of the command "be filled" could be illustrated by a common activity we all do: we fill up our cars at the gas station. When the tank cannot hold any more, the pump shuts off, and we pay for the gas.

---

[1] οἶνος (pron. OY nŏs)

[2] See William F. Arndt and F. Wilbur Gingrich, *A Greek-English Lexicon of the New Testament and Other Early Christian Literature* (Chicago: The University of Chicago Press, 1957), s.v. μεθύσκω, 500. The verb form in Eph. 5:18 is a present passive imperative. A. T. Robertson notes that "in general μή is used with the present imper. to forbid what one is already doing." *A Grammar of the Greek New Testament in the Light of Historical Research* (Nashville: Broadman, 1934), 890.

Someone might object that this analogy falls short of picturing the filling of the Spirit. After all, how can a person have a limited capacity for the Spirit's presence and influence in his life? The answer appears in a verse that is entirely parallel to the wider context of Ephesians 5:18. In Colossians 3:16 Paul commands believers, "Let the word of Christ dwell in you richly in all wisdom."[3] The two verses considered together indicate that our capacity for being filled with the Spirit is limited by how much of His word we can internalize. Ephesians 5:18 forbids consuming wine in sufficiently large quantities to become drunk,[4] but the second half of the verse, in combination with Colossians 3:16, commends taking in as much of the Scripture as we can hold.

Oinos Must Be Consumed in Moderation

Because of the potential for causing drunkenness, the New Testament authors mandate moderation in the consumption of wine. It was particularly important for leaders in the church to set a good example in moderation. Paul instructed Timothy that deacons must "be grave, not doubletongued, not given to much wine" (1 Tim. 3:8). The verb translated "given" is a present participle from the Greek verb προσέχω (*prosecho*). The general semantic idea of this verb is "turn one's mind to" something. It is used in 1 Timothy 3:8 to describe the action of paying too much attention to

---

[3]Both Eph. 5:18 and Col. 3:16 begin longer sections that develop exactly the same themes, often in nearly synonymous fashion. Being filled with the Spirit and letting the word of Christ dwell in us richly produce a song in our hearts, thanksgiving, submission of the wife to her husband, love of the husband toward his wife, obedience of children to parents, proper service toward masters, and equitable treatment of servants. It seems proper to conclude that being filled with the Spirit is equivalent to letting the word of Christ dwell in us richly.

[4]John MacArthur states that becoming intoxicated "would have required consuming a large quantity" of wine that had been diluted with water. "The wine of Bible times was not the same as the unmixed wine of our own day. Even the more civilized pagans of Bible times would have considered the drinking of modern wines to be barbaric and irresponsible." *The MacArthur New Testament Commentary: Ephesians* (Chicago: Moody Press, 1986), 237.

wine—to having an addiction for it.[5] The qualification deals not so much with the physical craving for alcohol as with the mental preoccupation with it. The term is reminiscent of Solomon's injunction against gazing at wine when it is red and sparkles in the cup (Prov. 23:31). The deacon must not have an inordinate affection for something the devil could use to enslave him.

In the case of the overseer, Paul states the qualification of moderate use of wine using slightly different terminology. Paul says that the overseer must not be "given to wine" (1 Tim. 3:3). This phrase translates the Greek adjective πάροινος (*paroinos*), literally "alongside wine." The word describes a person who has become a drunken addict.[6] It seems startling to us that Paul would have to specifically exclude a person like this from being the pastor of a church, but such lack of self-control is a danger in any era of history or cultural context.[7] In his book *Freedom from Addiction* Mike Quarles recounts the story of his struggle with alcoholism, even after his salvation while he was a counselor to alcoholics! He knew he was a hypocrite, but his life became a pattern of drunkenness, confession, sobriety for a while, and then back to drunkenness. He tried every program and organization he could find to break the hold that alcohol had on him. Finally the Lord gave him deliverance, but his story illustrates the reality that even someone in active ministry can be dominated by addiction to alcohol.[8]

---

[5]See Arndt and Gingrich, s.v. προσέχω, 721.

[6]R. C. H. Lenski notes that "a πάροινος is one who lingers long beside his wine, a winebibber, a tippler." *The Interpretation of St. Paul's Epistles to the Colossians, to the Thessalonians, to Timothy, to Titus and to Philemon* (Minneapolis: Augsburg, 1937), 585.

[7]It comes as no surprise, then, that when Paul prescribes (perhaps with the agreement of his frequent companion, Dr. Luke) wine as a medicinal response to Timothy's chronic stomach problems (1 Tim. 5:23), he specifies "a little" (ὀλίγος) quantity of the substance.

[8]Neil T. Anderson and Mike & Julia Quarles, *Freedom from Addiction: Breaking the Bondage of Addiction and Finding Freedom in Christ* (Ventura, CA: Regal Books,

The Scripture also enjoins women to be moderate in their consumption of wine. Paul told Titus to instruct older women to be "in behaviour as becometh holiness, not false accusers, not given to much wine" (Titus 2:3). Here the word given is the Greek perfect passive participle from δουλόω (*douloō*), a word that describes enslavement to something.[9] It is possible for Christian women to be enslaved to alcohol. Perhaps a woman would start drinking to excess as a way of dealing with stress and disappointment. What began as an escape valve could then escalate into full alcoholism. Such a condition would be the polar opposite of holy living.

Oinos Points to Spiritual Realities

The New Testament contains not only negative warnings concerning drunkenness but also a positive use of wine as a symbol for certain spiritual realities. At times our Savior used wine and the daily experience of drinking it to illustrate truth. In Matthew 11:1–19, for example, Christ instructed the crowd assembled around Him about who John the Baptist was. He said, "Among them that are born of women there hath not risen a greater than John the Baptist" (v. 11). But even this great prophet didn't suit the generation of Christ's day. Jesus viewed the people as little children who were never satisfied with God's messengers.[10] These fickle children could

---

1996). Anyone considering the idea that Christian liberty allows him to consume alcoholic beverages should read this book. Not only does Mike recount the devastation that alcohol brought into his life, but his wife also offers her perspective with such honesty that I came nearly to the point of tears several times in my reading.

[9]See Arndt and Gingrich, s.v. δουλόω, 205. D. Edmond Hiebert notes that the pairing of the two negatives in this verse, "not slanderers, not enslaved to much wine," suggests a close connection between gossip and having too much to drink. "Titus," in *The Expositor's Bible Commentary*, ed. Frank E. Gaebelein (Grand Rapids: Zondervan, 1978), 11:436.

[10]William Hendriksen states the matter well: "It is clear that Jesus is here accusing these critics of being childish. There is a difference between being childlike and being childish." *New Testament Commentary: Exposition of the Gospel According to Matthew* (Grand Rapids: Baker, 1973), 491.

not decide whether dancing to flute music was more fun than mourning to funeral music (vv. 16–17). Nothing pleased them. When John lived an ascetic lifestyle, the crowd was displeased that he was very different from them and deemed him possessed by a demon (v. 18). But when Christ came eating and drinking, just like a normal Israelite, the crowd accused Him of being a glutton and a drunkard! (v. 19). We can hardly imagine the grief such an assertion must have caused our sinless Savior.

The spiritual reality that Christ sought to impress on the hearts of His hearers is the identification and closeness of the Lamb of God with the people He came to redeem. Even though the crowd meant it in a pejorative sense, it is indeed true that Christ is "a friend of publicans and sinners" (Matt. 11:19b). We can all rejoice in that truth. John the Baptist's diet consisted of locusts and honey, but Christ ate the same food and drank the same everyday wine as did the typical person of His day. He was so completely identified with those He came to redeem that 700 years previously the prophet Isaiah had even called Him "Israel" (Isa. 49:3). John the Baptist lived as a Nazirite out in desolate places, but Jesus lived with the multitudes, submitted perfectly to the same demands of the Mosaic law in force for every Jewish person, and took the sins of the world upon Himself as He died on the cross.

Christ also used wine to represent a new, spiritual life that was vastly superior to the old, Pharisaic attempt at achieving personal righteousness through fastidious adherence to what they thought the law required. Christ never denigrated the Mosaic covenant. He even stated that not the smallest letter, or even the smallest part of a letter, would pass from the law until it was fulfilled (Matt. 5:18). Jesus often took the Pharisees to task, however, for their misunderstanding of the law as a vehicle for self-righteousness. They did not understand the true internal intent of various stipulations. They thought, for instance, that as long as they didn't murder some-one they had fulfilled the law's demand. Christ declared that the Pharisees were gravely mistaken, for the intent of the stipulation went right to the heart: someone so angry with his brother that he would like to kill him is guilty of violating the commandment (Matt. 5:21–22).

The Pharisees misunderstood the nature of fasting. They thought there was something meritorious in denying oneself proper nour-ishment. Under the influence of Pharisaic teaching, the disciples of John came to Christ and asked Him why His disciples never fasted (Matt. 9:14). Christ answered that the bridegroom's atten-dants do not fast at such a joyous occasion as a wedding! (v. 15). A new day has arrived for God's people, a time of joyful union between God and believers. Christ used two illustrations of the in-congruity of this new relationship compared with the old Pharisaic legalism. No one would sew a patch of new cloth on an old gar-ment, because the new material had not been pre-shrunk. As soon as someone washed the garment, the new material would cause a tear that was worse than the original defect the patch had repaired (v. 16). Then Christ declared, "Nor do men put new wine into old wineskins; otherwise the wineskins burst, and the wine pours out, and the wineskins are ruined; but they put new wine into fresh wineskins, and both are preserved" (NASB). Only new wineskins have the elasticity to expand as the new wine continues to undergo the process of fermentation and production of carbon-dioxide gas. If a person were to put new wine into stiff, old wineskins, they would tear, resulting in the loss of both wine and wineskins (v. 17). The new wine is a symbol for the joy and blessing of a true relationship with Christ in contrast to the burdensome legalism of the Pharisees.[11]

This same symbolism appears in John's account of the first miracle Jesus performed: transformation of water into wine during the wedding feast at Cana of Galilee (John 2:1–11). The biblical text implies that Jesus' mother Mary was probably related to either the bride or the groom, since the narrative opens with the information that she "was there" (v. 1).[12] Jesus was invited, and along with Him came the disciples as well (v. 2). Sometime after their arrival, or perhaps even because their presence put an additional drain on the provisions of the feast, Mary announced to Jesus that there was no more wine (v. 3). To the modern reader this situation seems to be a minor inconvenience, but it was a significant embarrassment to the groom.[13]

Mary's report to Jesus about this sad turn of events was most likely a veiled request to do something about it. Jesus' response to His own mother sounds harsh to our ears, but the vocative use of *woman* was actually a form of tender address: "Woman, what have I to do with thee?" (v. 4).[14] This phrase, literally "what to me and to you," was used in the Old Testament idiomatically to express the idea "leave me alone." R. V. G. Tasker suggests that

---

[11]Colin Brown summarizes the illustration of new wine in old wineskins by observing that "the Pharisaic outlook is burst apart by the life that he [Christ] brings." "Vine, Wine," in *The New International Dictionary of New Testament Theology*, ed. Colin Brown (Grand Rapids: Zondervan, 1978), 3:921.

[12]The Greek verb translated *was* (in the imperfect tense) implies Mary's presence during the preparations for the wedding before Jesus arrived. There is a contrast between this imperfect and the aorist tense that describes how Jesus had been invited. See Leon Morris, *The Gospel According to John*, in The New International Commentary on the New Testament, ed. F. F. Bruce (Grand Rapids: Eerdmans, 1971), 178, note 10. The assistance Mary rendered would be indicative of something a close relative or friend would do.

[13]Morris, 179.

[14]B. F. Westcott, *The Gospel According to St. John* (1881, rpt. ed.; Grand Rapids: Eerdmans, 1978), 36.

the sense here in John 2:4 is "your concern and mine are not the same."[15] Mary was focused on rescuing the groom from his immediate lack of provision for the feast, but Christ was concerned with man's lack of what wine pictures: the joy and provision of new life in Him. Christ's focus in His earthly ministry was always on His coming vicarious death, which would provide imputed righteousness for mankind. When our Savior talked with the woman of Samaria, for example, she could think only of quenching her physical thirst with water from the well. Our Savior, however, was thinking about what water pictured: "But whosoever drinketh of the water that I shall give him shall never thirst; but the water that I shall give him shall be in him a well of water springing up into everlasting life" (John 4:14).

Christ spent His whole life in single-hearted preparation for His hour, His work on the cross that would propitiate the just wrath of God on the sin of man.[16] When our Savior said to Mary, "Mine hour is not yet come" (John 2:4), perhaps He was meditating on the way wine was an appropriate picture of the blood He would shed. Indeed the night before the crucifixion He would say to His disciples as He took the cup of the Passover celebration in His hand, "Drink ye all of it; For this is my blood of the new testament, which is shed for many for the remission of sins" (Matt. 26:27–28).

Undeterred by Jesus' hesitance to address the immediate situation at the wedding feast, Mary commanded the servants, "Whatso-

---

[15]R. V. G. Tasker, *The Gospel According to St. John: An Introduction and Commentary*, vol. 4 of *Tyndale New Testament Commentaries*, ed. R. V. G. Tasker (Grand Rapids: Eerdmans, 1960), 60.

[16]Tasker observes, "It is impossible to interpret the words *mine hour* on the lips of Jesus without reference to other passages in the Gospel where 'the hour' invariably refers to the hour of the passion. The certainty that one day that hour would strike would seem to have conditioned, directly or indirectly, all that Jesus said or did in preparation for it" (56).

ever he saith unto you, do it" (John 2:5). John is careful at this point in the narrative to inform the reader that there were six stone waterpots nearby that the Jews used for their ceremonial washing, each with a capacity of twenty to thirty gallons. It was the custom of the Pharisees to wash their hands very carefully before every meal with water from pots like these. Later in our Savior's dealings with the Pharisees, He would offend them by His failure to observe their manmade ordinances. In Mark 7:1–13, Christ strongly reproved the Pharisees about their elevation of traditional ordinances above the Word of God. They were more concerned with washing their hands than they were with obeying the command of the Decalogue to honor their parents. The waterpots at the wedding feast, therefore, were a visible reminder of the Pharisees' perversion of the Scripture and their self-righteous, fastidious devotion to manmade religion.

Now Christ commanded the servants to fill these waterpots to the brim (John 2:7). John does not inform the reader how full the pots were before the servants topped them off. Christ instructs the servants to draw water from the pots and take it to the governor of the feast (v. 8). Somewhere between the pots and the governor, something miraculous happened: Christ transformed the water into wine. A process that would normally take an entire growing season happened instantaneously. Christ bypassed absorption of water from the ground by grapevines, the production of grapes, harvesting by the vineyard workers, stomping of the grapes by barefoot workers, and fermentation in the wine vat.

When the governor of the feast tasted the wine, he was amazed. Normally a bridegroom would bring out his very best vintage at the start of the wedding celebration. Then, after the guests had consumed enough wine to be past the point of discernment,[17] the bridegroom would bring out the cheaper wine. The governor could not understand why this bridegroom had saved the best wine until last (John 2:9–10). By turning the water in pots used for Pharisaic rituals into the best wine, Christ was showing the superiority of His life-giving, atoning blood over the dead legalism of the Pharisees. Christ manifested His glory through this wonderful miracle (v. 11).

I am aware that many interpreters insist that the wine Christ created was non-alcoholic. John MacArthur, for example, states quite plainly, "It seems hard to believe that the wine Jesus miraculously made at the wedding feast in Cana or that He served at the Lord's Supper and on other occasions was fermented. How could He have made or served that which had even the potential for making a person drunk?" (237). Some use as evidence of this position the statement that those at the wedding feast had already "well drunk" (v. 10); would Christ have given more fermented wine to people who had already consumed a significant amount? I have no desire to pick a fight with my brethren over this issue, but I maintain that an objective reading of the narrative strongly supports the conclusion that Christ made a fermented product. As an exegete I am bound by what the Scripture actually says, not by what I wish it might say. The governor of the feast was no doubt an expert on wine. He deemed the quality of the water-turned-wine better than (not a different beverage from) the wine already served. Because the governor stated that the wine already consumed had intoxicating potential, the logical conclusion is that the wine Jesus made was alcoholic. No doubt this wine was diluted with water before

---

[17]The governor of the feast says that normally every man serves the good wine first, καὶ ὅταν μεθυσθῶσιν ("and when they have become drunk") the cheaper quality wine gets served. The verb μεθύσκω is the same one Paul uses in Eph. 5:18 to express the idea of becoming drunk.

people drank it (as was the custom of the day), but it had the potential to cause drunkenness if abused. In answer to the question of how Christ could make something alcoholic, one needs to observe only that as Creator our Savior made the very process of fermentation. There is nothing inherently wrong with wine, just as there is nothing intrinsically wrong with anything Christ created. He also created the poppy plant, from which man can make pain-killing morphine or life-ruining heroin. It is man who bears the responsibility for abusing the good gifts God gives to us.

Oinos Is a Picture of Sin and God's Judgment

Wine is not a static metaphor in the New Testament; it can picture God's judgment as well as aspects of His salvation. Wine fits the role of portraying the disastrous consequences of God's wrath on sin because drunkenness has such deleterious effects on a human being. It is no wonder, therefore, that wine in the book of Revelation stands for sin and the judgment God brings to bear on mankind. In Revelation 14:8 an angel announces, "Babylon is fallen, is fallen, that great city, because she made all nations drink of the wine of the wrath of her fornication." This announcement is a combination of two Old Testament prophecies. Isaiah declared, "Babylon is fallen, is fallen" (21:9), a repetition that emphasizes the certainty and completeness of the city's destruction. The prophet Jeremiah wrote, "Babylon hath been a golden cup in the Lord's hand, that made all the earth drunken: the nations have drunken of her wine [*yayin*]; therefore the nations are mad" (51:7).

All the nations had been willing participants in the wicked religion of worshiping the Antichrist, and all had joined his political and economic empire. John portrays their participation in the Antichrist's kingdom as getting drunk with wine because the nations have joined in a crazy satanic rebellion against the sovereign rule of God that any sober person would avoid. All the nations that have participated in worshiping the beast "shall drink of the wine of the wrath of God, which is poured out without mixture into the cup of his indignation" (Rev. 14:10). Only barbaric people drank full-strength wine in John's day,[18] but sinners will consume God's wrath undiluted. God's anger involves eternal torment with fire and brimstone, allowing no rest day or night forever (vv. 10–11).

GLEUKOS[19]

The second Greek term the New Testament authors use for wine is the noun *gleukos*, a word used only in Acts 2:13. The setting involves the events of the day of Pentecost. Jews had come from all over the Roman world to worship in Jerusalem, and they spoke many different languages. The disciples, who were together in one place, were suddenly filled with the Holy Spirit and began speaking in the different languages of the people who had come to Jerusalem. These foreigners were completely mystified that uneducated Galileans had the ability to communicate in so many languages. But not everyone was amazed. Some observers took this opportunity to impugn the disciples by claiming, "These men are full of new wine" (Acts 2:13). "New wine" is the translation of the Greek word *gleukos*. This was wine that had undergone the initial phase of fermentation but still had a fairly high sugar content. Apparently it was intoxicating if consumed in large enough quantities, because the mocking crowd sought to explain the disciples' miraculous speech by asserting they were simply drunk. Peter dispelled their mistaken idea by noting that it was only 9 AM, far too early in the day for anyone to be drunk (Acts 2:15).

---

[18]Amerine states the matter bluntly: "Only barbarians drank undiluted wine." "Wine," 23:518.

[19]γλεῦκος (pron. GLOO kōs)

CONCLUSION

Just like the Old Testament words for alcoholic beverages, the New Testament words *oinos* and *gleukos* refer to an alcoholic beverage that must be used in moderation. Violation of the principle of moderate use of wine disqualified a person from holding a position of leadership in the church. Older women also needed to be very careful how much they imbibed, because younger women looked to them as examples of Christian virtue.

Wine is also used in the New Testament as a symbol for the spiritual blessings of salvation that God offers in Christ. Because Christ drank the *vin ordinaire* of the common people, wine became a picture of his closeness with the people He came to redeem. In the parable of the wineskins and the miracle of the water turned into wine, Christ portrayed the new life He offered through His shed blood as superior to the Pharisaic attempt at earning personal righteousness through fastidious adherence to manmade religion.

In a striking contrast with elements of salvation, wine is also used as a metaphor of God's wrath on sin. The book of Revelation portrays sinners in the eschatological future drinking wine from the undiluted cup of God's wrath. The variable nature of wine as a metaphor of either judgment or salvation is completely congruous with the consumption of wine in either moderation or excess.

3

HISTORICAL VIEWS OF
ALCOHOL CONSUMPTION

As we have seen in our examination of the biblical words for alcoholic beverages, the Scripture commends the moderate use of these hydrating drinks and condemns drunkenness. The main error that a modern interpreter might make, however, is assuming that modern alcoholic beverages are equivalent to those consumed in biblical days. A key component of exegesis is an analysis of cultural elements in the original setting of the Scripture that may differ from our setting today.[1] A view of the historic use of alcoholic beverages indicates that what ancient people drank was far less intoxicating than modern drinks. Putting this concept into the words of the modern proverb, we must be careful to compare apples to apples—not apples to oranges. In formulating our standards of Christian conduct, we must recognize that it is much easier to become intoxicated by drinking modern alcoholic beverages than it was by drinking wine in ancient days. Maynard A. Amerine notes,

> The wine of classical antiquity, however, was very different from modern wine. Both Greeks and Romans lined storage vessels with resin, which imbued the wine with its taste. They often flavored their wine heavily with spices, herbs, flowers, and perfume, and always diluted it with

---

[1]For more information on cultural analysis, see Walter C. Kaiser, Jr., *Toward an Exegetical Theology: Biblical Exegesis for Preaching and Teaching* (Grand Rapids: Baker, 1981), 114–21.

water before consumption, probably to dilute the strong flavoring. *Only barbarians drank undiluted wine.*[2]

We find in a broad historical survey of alcohol consumption, from classical Greece to our current cultural context, that the further history progresses, the less awareness there is that "only barbarians drank undiluted wine."

DRINKING IN GREECE AND ROME

Because the climate and soil of the Mediterranean region is conducive to viticulture, wine became an essential aspect of Greco-Roman culture. We know quite a bit from extant literature and art about their drinking. "Both in Greece and in Italy wine, which (except in ritual and as medicine) was almost always diluted with water, formed part of the staple diet, and even slaves were allowed their ration."[3]

According to Charles Seltman, the Greeks actually preferred pure water to drink. Certain wells and springs were prized for their cold mineral waters, but a person had to travel to the source in order to enjoy this exceptional treat. Most water from the typical well or cistern, however, was probably contaminated and could easily cause sickness. The ancient Greeks sought a safe source of hydration, and wine became the beverage of choice. After the grapes of the harvest had been trodden, the juice was placed in *pithoi,* large jars with bell-shaped mouths that would allow the carbon dioxide from the fermentation process to escape. The *gleukos* (grape juice) would undergo rapid fermentation for a little over a week. Often some *hepsema,* juice that had been boiled down to a consistency of jelly, would be added to the *pithoi* in order to increase the sugar

---

[2]Amerine, "Wine," 23:518 (emphasis added).

[3]N. G. L. Hammond and H. H. Scullard, eds., *The Oxford Classical Dictionary,* 2nd ed. (London: Oxford University Press, 1970), s.v. "Wine," 1138.

content (and, hence, the percentage of ethanol in the finished product). Once covered, the *pithoi* were set aside until the following spring. Wine would then be transferred for distribution in an *amphora*, an oval-shaped vessel with large handles on each side.[4]

Wine with an alcoholic content greater than nine percent would stay fresh in an *amphora* indefinitely. When needed for consumption, wine would be measured into a large mixing bowl, called a *krater*, along with water. The dilution factor varied, but the most popular recipe was one part wine to three parts water. At this ratio the alcoholic content was approximately 2–3%. A person could attend an extended feast, drinking as his thirst would dictate, and never become intoxicated by a beverage containing such a low amount of alcohol. Seltman maintains that "it is always a matter of surprise to learn how constantly the ancient Greeks mixed water with their wine."[5]

DRINKING IN JEWISH CULTURE

At this point in our study we make the assumption that if the Greeks considered the consumption of undiluted wine to be barbaric, the Jews would not have been less sensitive to the potential dissipation that undiluted wine could produce. We wish the Bible contained explicit statements about how wine was consumed (similar to what we have in reference to Grecian culture), but we find none. We do have a record of Jewish customs of drinking, however, preserved in the Talmud.

The word *Talmud* means "instruction" and comes from the Hebrew verb *to teach*. The Talmud consists of two main divisions: the Hebrew *Mishnah* (completed about AD 200) and the Aramaic

---

[4]Charles Seltman, *Wine in the Ancient World* (London: Routledge & Kegan Paul Ltd., 1957), 67–71.

[5]Ibid., 91.

Gemara (the Babylonian Gemara was finished by AD 500). The Mishnah contains both oral tradition purportedly given by Moses and detailed explanations of the Scriptures presented in six orders: agriculture, feasts, women, civil and criminal law, sacrifices, and unclean things. These orders are further divided into 63 tractates. The Gemara contains a more detailed commentary on various aspects of the Mishnah.[6]

It is uncertain exactly how much water was used in Jewish society when wine was diluted. There was probably no set amount, the dilution ratio being determined solely by the personal preference of the drinker. Wine was probably expensive for the average Israelite, so the greater the dilution, the more economical the beverage became. One view maintains that during the Talmudic period "it was customary to dilute wine before drinking by adding one-third water."[7] The second order of the Mishnah, however, gives a different dilution ratio in the first of its twelve tractates, entitled "Sabbath."[8] In this tractate we find rules for the quantities of various beverages that must not be carried about on the Sabbath. When it comes to wine, a Jewish person was not to carry "sufficient wine in a goblet, which with the addition of a certain quantity of water would make a full goblet of wine (fit to drink)."[9] Various rabbis argued (as they did about almost everything!) whether the dilution ratio should be one part wine to three parts water or one part wine to two parts water.[10] Whatever the dilution ratio was, it is apparent that Jewish

---

[6]See Gleason L. Archer, *A Survey of Old Testament Introduction*, rev. ed. (Chicago: Moody, 1994), 70.

[7]Geoffrey Wigoder, ed., *The New Encyclopedia of Judaism* (Washington Square: New York University Press, 2002), s.v. "Wine," 799.

[8]See Hermann L. Strack, *Introduction to the Talmud and Midrash* (Philadelphia: Jewish Publication Society of America, 1931), 34–35.

[9]Michael L. Rodkinson, *New Edition of the Babylonian Talmud*, 2nd ed. (Boston: New Talmud Publishing Company, 1903), 1:143.

[10]Ibid., 143–44.

people, like the Greeks, did not consider the consumption of un-diluted wine to be proper.[11]

THE LORD'S TABLE IN THE EARLY CHURCH

Because the early church was composed of many Jewish con-verts and quickly spread into Greece, it is not surprising that the Lord's Supper was observed with wine that had been mixed with water. Church Fathers such as Ignatius of Antioch (c. AD 35–110) strongly emphasized the importance of a church unity that was enhanced by the frequent observance of Communion. Cyprian (d. 258) agreed with Ignatius:

> The union of believers with Christ in the Eucharist is also stressed by St. Cyprian of Carthage who, speaking of the mixing of water and wine in the cup, gives an extended meaning to this mixing: "The people are designated by water, the blood of Christs [sic] by wine. Mixing water and wine in the cup shows the people's union with Christ, the believers' union with Him in Whom they believe. Water and wine after mixing in the Lord's Cup are so inseparably and closely united that they cannot be separated one from another. In just this way nothing can separate from Christ the Church, that is, the people that make up the Church, firmly and unshakeably abiding in faith and joined by eternal, indivisible love."[12]

---

[11]"Wine was rarely consumed undiluted in first-century C.E. Israel. So the Book of Maccabees recommends: 'Just as it is harmful to drink wine alone, or, again, to drink water alone . . . wine mixed with water is sweet and delicious and enhances one's enjoy-ment' (2 Maccabees 15:39)." Michael M. Homan and Mark A. Gstohl, "Jesus the Tee-totaler: How Dr. Welch Put the Lord on the Wagon," *Bible Review* 18 (April 2002), 29.

[12]A Monk of St. Tikhon's Monastery, ed., *These Truths We Hold: The Holy Ortho-dox Church: Her Life and Teachings* (South Canaan, PA: St. Tikhon's Seminary Press, 1986), 304.

Although someone might object that Cyprian may have gotten a bit fanciful in his identification of imagery, his view is important for our study because of his commitment to the use of diluted wine in Communion.

THE USE OF ALCOHOLIC BEVERAGES BY THE REFORMERS

By the time of the Reformation, however, a recognition of the importance of avoiding undiluted alcoholic beverages seems to have been lost. In Luther's day excessive drinking in Germany had reached epidemic proportions. Although he spoke more vehemently against drunkenness than any of his contemporaries, Luther drank alcoholic beverages in moderation without a qualm.[13]

> In fact, Luther as an advocate of prohibition would be as much an unhistorical fantasy as Luther the drunkard. When in August, 1540, he says: "I drink also, but not every person ought to try and imitate me," when he says that God ought to give him credit for occasionally taking a good draught in his honor, and when he writes to a melancholiac: "I frequently drink more copiously in order to vex the devil," this all proves sufficiently that Luther was by no means averse to a good drink.[14]

That a man of Luther's standing would not avoid participating in an activity that had obviously enslaved many of his fellow Germans is difficult to understand. He does seem sensitive to the example he was setting ("not every person ought to try and imitate me"), but his conscience apparently did not bother him enough to produce a repudiation of alcohol.

---

[13]Heinrich Böhmer, *Luther in Light of Recent Research*, trans. Carl F Huth, Jr. (New York: The Christian Herald, 1916), 206–8.

[14]Ibid., 213.

The same was true of Calvin. He viewed food and drink as a gift from God to be enjoyed by all men. As did Luther, Calvin gave great importance to moderation.

> "It is permissible to use wine," he argued, "not only for necessity, but also to make us merry." Christ's provision of an abundance of "most excellent wine" at the wedding in Cana was proof enough of its goodness. Only two conditions should govern wine-drinking: first that it be moderate, "lest men forget themselves, drown their senses, and destroy their strength"; and second, that, "in making merry," they feel a livelier gratitude to God.[15]

The Reformers did not view drinking alcoholic beverages, therefore, as simply a necessary means of hydration. They insisted that drinking, along with good food, produced social enjoyment and an occasion for redeemed man to praise God for His good gifts.

SOCIAL ASPECTS OF DRINKING IN COLONIAL AMERICA

Because many of the early colonists who came to New England were Puritans, they brought with them the Reformers' views about consuming alcoholic beverages.

> Puritans had a straightforward attitude toward alcohol: moderate use was good; immoderate use was evil. Most of their European contemporaries shared this view in the seventeenth century, and most of the western world still does today. Thus, in abstract terms, the morality concerning the consumption of alcohol posed no problems to Puritan ideology. Used in an appropriate manner alcohol was socially beneficial, relaxing, sanctioned by Scripture, even healthy. Used in an inappropriate manner, it destroyed body and

---

[15]William J. Bouwsma, *John Calvin: A Sixteenth-Century Portrait* (London: Oxford University Press, 1988), 136.

soul, ravaged the family and community, and was an abomination in the eyes of God and the commonwealth.[16]

During their voyage to America on the *Mayflower*, the Puritans, even their little children, drank beer. Consumption of water was viewed by most Englishmen as a very unwise practice, due to the contamination of most sources. Once they were in America, beer continued to be the beverage of choice for most male New Englanders, although cider eventually became quite popular due to the ease of its production and its relatively low alcoholic content. Although drinking beer was common at home, taverns began to appear widely during the 1660s. Until this time drunkenness had not been a significant problem in New England. Each community guarded itself carefully to ensure that drinking didn't get out of hand, and penalties for inebriation were stiff. Taverns (known originally as "ordinaries") were more difficult to police. Various laws were enacted to regulate what took place in taverns, but by the eighteenth century an alehouse culture developed that caused many Puritan leaders alarm. Other New Englanders considered taverns to be an important place of social interaction and relaxation. Because there were no hotels for travelers, even those who spoke against taverns would find themselves staying in one overnight for lack of alternative lodging.[17]

THE TEMPERANCE MOVEMENT IN AMERICA

Nineteenth-century America experienced some highly significant changes. Probably the most important was the migration of rural farmers into industrial urban centers of commerce and prosperity. The population of the nation's cities exploded, especially as millions of European immigrants swelled the ranks of new urbanites

---

[16]Bruce C. Daniels, *Puritans at Play: Leisure and Recreation in Colonial America* (New York: St. Martin's Press, 1995), 141.

[17]Ibid., 142–59.

from the farm seeking a better life and enjoyment. Now there was no influence from a concerned local pastor in a small, rural church to encourage people in a lifestyle of temperance concerning the use of alcoholic beverages. Along with the increase of population in America's cities came large quantities of distilled liquor dispensed at ubiquitous bars. One-hundred-proof whiskey is 50% ethanol, ten times (or more) as intoxicating as the beer that had been popular in colonial days.

Intoxication became a horrible problem in America's urban areas. Drunkenness ruined people's health, cost them the money that should have gone to feed their wives and children, fueled crimes of every sort, and caused loss of productivity at work. Christian leaders began to notice the cultural disaster that was unfolding before their eyes. Pastors started to preach on the sin of drunkenness, and many of them banded together to work in concert against this menace that was blighting the lives of so many. Thus the temperance movement was born.

Perhaps John Wesley was the first high-profile leader to take a stand against "spirituous liquors" (distilled alcohol products). In 1743 he included drunkenness, buying or selling distilled liquor, or drinking these intoxicants as sins to be avoided by the members of his societies. In 1777 the Continental Congress passed a resolution encouraging each legislative body in the United States to ban the production of liquor. The first formal temperance group in America, "The Union Temperate Society of Moreau and Northumberland," was founded in 1808. This was a local movement that encouraged its members to refrain from drinking liquor. The first national organization was formed in 1826 in Boston. The American Temperance Society sought to advance its stand against liquor with a nationwide campaign. Also in 1826 Lyman Beecher published his *Six Sermons on Temperance*. These messages stirred people from lethargy to an active opposition to liquor. The movement was now poised to make significant gains in membership and national influence.[18]

In 1833 the temperance movement changed from one of combating liquor to a force for total abstinence from *all* alcoholic beverages. People began to realize that former alcoholics who had recovered from addiction to liquor were being ensnared by beer and wine. So in May of 1833, the American Temperance Union was inaugurated in Philadelphia to promote total abstinence. Over the next forty years the temperance movement sought legislative means on the state and local levels to ban the distribution or sale of liquor, beer, and wine. There were many victories as well as defeats.[19] Temperance advocates realized that the ultimate solution could come only on the federal level.

The Anti-Saloon League, formed in 1895, became the most effective organization for putting pressure on legislators at the national level. This organization maintained that, by conservative estimate, 19% of divorces, 25% of poverty, 25% of insanity, 37% of pauperism, 45% of child desertion, and 50% of all crime in America were directly attributable to alcohol consumption. Various scientific and medical studies were published in the early twentieth century that aided the Anti-Saloon League's cause by dispelling many of the myths people had long held concerning the supposed health benefits of alcohol. Even wealthy industrialists funded the League because of their concern over alcohol's effects in lost productivity and absenteeism. The DuPonts, Rockefellers, Wanamakers, and

---

[18]John M'Clintock and James Strong, *Cyclopaedia of Biblical, Theological, and Ecclesiastical Literature* (New York: Harper, 1891), 10:245–46.

[19]Ibid., 246–49.

Kresges contributed generously toward the League's annual $2.5 million budget.[20]

The Anti-Saloon League might never have been successful in its quest toward prohibition, though, without the events of the First World War. Just before the war many German brewing companies allied themselves with the German-American Alliance, an organization that sought to preserve the heritage of German immigrants in the U.S. and oppose any legislative actions adversely affecting the beer industry. Such an alliance was a bad move for companies with names that were obviously German, such as Pabst, Schlitz, and Blatz. Foes of the beer industry capitalized on the extremely negative feelings many Americans had toward the imperialistic ambitions of the Kaiser. As the war progressed, these German brewers were pictured as the murderers of American servicemen and as scoundrels for using precious resources that should have gone into the war effort. "In 1917, the resolution to prohibit the manufacture, sale, transportation or importation of alcoholic beverages in the United States was approved by Congress and sent to the states for ratification. It took only one year and eight days for the 18th Amendment to secure the necessary ratification."[21]

Our Bible-believing forebears contributed significantly to the fight against the misery, domestic abuse, poverty, crime, and loss of health that alcohol abuse causes. Evangelist Billy Sunday preached to approximately 80–100 million people during a career that spanned the years 1896–1935.[22] Sunday was dead set against the liquor industry:

---

[20]Jane Lang McGrew, "History of Alcohol Prohibition," available at http://www.druglibrary.org/Schaffer/LIBRARY/studies/nc/nc2a.htm; accessed August 10, 2007.

[21]Ibid.

[22]William A. "Billy" Sunday, *The Sawdust Trail: Billy Sunday in His Own Words*, foreword by Robert F. Martin (Iowa City: University of Iowa Press, 2005), vii.

I am the sworn, eternal and uncompromising enemy of the liquor traffic and have been for thirty-five years. I saw that nine-tenths of the misery, poverty, wrecked homes and blighted lives were caused by booze. I saw it rob men of their manhood and clothe them in rags, take away their health, rob their families, incite the father to butcher his wife and child, rip the shirt off the back of a shivering man, take the last drop of milk from the breast of a nursing mother, send women to steaming over a washtub to manicure their finger nails to the quick to get money to feed the hungry brood, while it sent their father home from their hell holes, a bleary-eyed, bloated face, staggering, reeling, jabbering wreck while all hell screamed with delight and heaven wept and the angels hid behind their harps. I drew my sword and have never sheathed it, and never will as long as there is a distillery or brewery or a bootlegger or speak-easy on earth. I put twelve states dry before we voted on the Eighteenth Amendment.[23]

Sunday's words express the sentiment of a warrior for Christ. His stand against sin was never difficult to understand or camouflaged by esoteric nuances of expression. He meant what he said and said what he meant. It would be a shame if we, his heirs in the defense and propagation of the gospel, ever fail to issue just as clarion a call against the abuse of alcohol.

---

[23]Ibid., 68.

4

MEDICAL VIEWS OF ALCOHOL CONSUMPTION

Christians ought to care deeply about how they treat their bodies.[1] Because our bodies are the temple of the Holy Spirit (1 Cor. 6:19), we must make sure that we are not doing anything that would be deleterious to our long-term health. Sometimes medical science changes its conclusions about different issues related to nutrition and health. When I was growing up, the prevailing wisdom dictated the use of margarine instead of butter. Medical researchers later found that the trans-fats in margarine were injurious to heart health. Suddenly butter was back on the table. There are some matters, however, that are quite assured due to unassailable research and unanimous opinion. One such issue is smoking. Many statistical studies have identified smoking as the primary cause of several serious lung diseases, including lung cancer and chronic obstructive pulmonary disease (COPD). These ailments kill hundreds of thousands of people every year.[2] Smoking furthermore is well known to be a major contributor to many other cancers and to the cardiovascular disease process. The evidence is so overwhelming that only an extremely ill-informed or ill-willed person would deny the cause-and-effect relationship. These days it would be unusual to find a Christian who thinks he can smoke and still be a good steward of his body. On the other hand there

---

[1]This chapter was written in collaboration with Daniel T. Borkert, MD. I am indebted to him for his editorial review and addition of helpful material.

[2]American Lung Association, "Lung Disease Data at a Glance: Tobacco Use," available at http://www.lungusa.org/site/pp.asp?c=dvLUK9O0E&b=327861; accessed September 16, 2007.

seems to be no lack of believers who have concluded that consuming alcoholic beverages, at least in moderation, may even be beneficial to a person's health. An examination of the current views of medical researchers is necessary.

THE MEDICAL VIEW OF ALCOHOL ABUSE

Medical science has conducted extensive research on the health issues involved in drinking alcoholic beverages. Some conclusions about the effects of alcohol on the human body are certain, and some are more tentative. The most obvious and undeniable physiological effect is on brain function. Frequently when alcohol affects the way the brain functions, serious psychological problems will manifest themselves.

> For active alcoholics, drinking trumps reason. It distorts judgment. It severs the connection between behavior and consequence. It lays waste to marriages, friendships, and careers. It leaves children stranded. For alcoholics, love and logic can't hold a candle to liquor.[3]

Medical researchers are just beginning to understand the biochemical mechanisms that produce addiction to alcohol. Alcohol has the ability to affect the brain by stimulating centers of behavior and learning. In response to alcohol, the brain releases GABA, a neurotransmitter that produces powerful feelings of euphoria. At the same time the brain also releases glutamate, a factor to counterbalance the influence of GABA. Glutamate joins GABA in certain areas of the brain that control memory. In order to deal with excess amounts of glutamate, the brain responds by changing the structure of receptor cells, but habitual use of alcohol negates the brain's response. Eventually the combination of GABA and high

---

[3]Susan Brink, "Your Brain on Alcohol," available at http://www.usnews.com/usnews/culture/articles/010507/archive_001356_2.htm; posted April 29, 2001, accessed August 3, 2007.

levels of glutamate produce such strong memories of the euphoria of drinking that the alcohol abuser who has attempted to recover from his addiction may find an overwhelming urge to drink even years after he has avoided any alcoholic beverages.[4]

> Over the last decade, sophisticated brain-imaging technologies have demonstrated that constant use of alcohol significantly alters the structure of the brain in ways that can last for months and even years, creating a chronic brain disease.[5]

It is hard to imagine that anyone who abuses alcohol took his first drink with the specific goal of becoming an alcoholic. Indeed there is no way of predicting with any degree of certainty who might become an addict. There are approximately 18 million people in the United States who abuse or are addicted to alcohol (about 6% of the total population). Out of this total, only about 2 million alcohol abusers seek treatment each year, and about 90% of them will suffer a relapse within four years.[6]

Clearly the physiological and psychological effects of excessive alcohol consumption are horrendous. Each year 100,000 Americans die from alcohol-related problems.[7] More specifically, one-third of suicides, 50% of all homicides,[8] 40% of all traffic fatalities,[9] and between 48 and 68% of deaths from fire are the direct consequence

---

[4]Catherine Arnst, "Can Alcoholism Be Treated?" *Business Week* (April 11, 2005), 97.

[5]Ibid., 96.

[6]Ibid., 97.

[7]Mayo Clinic Staff, "Alcoholism," available at http://www.mayoclinic.com/health/alcoholism/DS00340; accessed September 3, 2007.

[8]"Sobering Facts on the Dangers of Alcohol," *NY Newsday*, April 24, 2002.

[9]National Highway Traffic Safety, Annual Report, 2006, available at www.nhtsa.dot.gov/portal/nhtsa_static_file_downloader.jsp?file=/staticfiles/DOT/NHTSA/NCSA/Content/RNotes/2007/810821.pdf; accessed September 16, 2007.

of alcohol impairment.[10] These statistics relate only the deaths involved—there are hundreds of thousands more who are injured through the use of this legal toxic substance. In fact one-fourth of all emergency-room admissions are related to alcohol.[11]

Besides trauma, many other harmful physical manifestations come from drinking alcohol. Many are aware of the gastro-intestinal diseases of hepatitis, gastritis, cirrhosis, and pancreatitis.[12] But excessive alcohol may also lead to the development of a number of other acute and chronic diseases. Many of the neurological problems of dementia, stroke, and neuropathies are the result of the abuse of alcoholic drink.[13] Some cardiac ailments, including myocardial infarction (heart attacks), cardiomyopathies, hypertension, and atrial fibrillation, are a direct consequence of excessive consumption of alcohol.[14] Finally, many cancers of the mouth, throat, esophagus, stomach, liver, prostate, and breast are linked to alcohol.[15] When the costs of medical treatment, lost wages, and law-enforcement resources are all added up, alcohol

[10]Position Paper on Drug Policy, Physician Leadership on National Drug Policy (PLNDP), Brown University Center for Alcohol and Addiction Studies, 2000.

[11]"Sobering Facts."

[12]Centers for Disease Control, "General Information on Alcohol Use and Health," available at http://www.cdc.gov/alcohol/quickstats/general_info.htm; accessed September 3, 2007.

[13]G. Carrao, L. Rubbiati, A. Zambon, C. La Vecchia, "A Meta-Analysis of Alcohol Consumption and the Risk of 15 Diseases," PrevMed 38 (2004): 613–19.

[14]J. Rehm, G. Gmel, C. T. Sepsos, M. Trevisan, "Alcohol-Related Morbidity and Mortality," Alcohol Research and Health 27, no. 1 (2003): 39–51.

[15]"Consumption of wine, beer, hard liquor, and all combined showed positive associations with neoplasms of the oral cavity, larynx, esophagus, colon, rectum, breast, and thyroid gland." R. R. Williams and J. W. Horm, "Association of Cancer Sites with Tobacco and Alcohol Consumption and Socioeconomic Status of Patients: Interview Study from the Third National Cancer Survey," abstract available at http://www.ncbi.nlm.nih.gov/sites/entrez?Db=pubmed&Cmd=ShowDetailView&TermToSearch=557114&ordinalpos=25&itool=EntrezSystem2.PEntrez.Pubmed.Pubmed_ResultsPanel.Pubmed_RVDocSum; accessed August 24, 2007.

addiction costs Americans $185 *billion* per year.[16] When considering all these facts together, any reasonable individual should be "sobered" to realize that drinking alcoholic beverages is not simply a social preference!

The economic costs are just a fraction of the misery. How can we quantify the grief a drunk driver has caused a family whose beloved relative has just been killed in a violent car crash? What value can we place on the life of a woman whose drunken husband just shot her dead in a fit of alcoholic rage? How can we assess the emotional trauma of a child who goes to bed each night terrified that his drunken parent might do him harm?

There is a strong genetic predisposition for alcohol addiction. Further, a Christian is just as susceptible to addiction as any unsaved person. The same biochemical factors that enslave unsaved people are at work in a Christian's brain when he drinks alcoholic beverages. It would be naïve for a believer to think that the Lord will somehow protect him from alcoholism simply because he knows the Lord as his Savior. Alcoholism is definitely a spiritual problem, and the Scripture repeatedly condemns it as sin (e.g., 1 Cor. 6:9–10). But alcoholism has the additional dangerous aspect of physical addiction as a factor. Drinking alcoholic beverages is the medical equivalent of playing Russian roulette with a real handgun loaded with real bullets.

THE MEDICAL VIEW OF MODERATE ALCOHOL CONSUMPTION

Research in the area of alcohol also indicates that *moderate* alcohol intake can actually be helpful in preventing cardiovascular disease. When alcohol is consumed at the proper dose, it appears, among other things, to raise good cholesterol (HDL), lower blood pressure,

---

[16]Arnst, 97.

and inhibit platelet function in accelerating arteriosclerosis. This cardio-protective effect is inherent to the ethanol molecule alone and is independent of the type of alcoholic beverage.[17]

Anyone who has been reading health-advice articles in magazines and newspapers has undoubtedly seen at least one presentation of the benefits of alcohol consumption. *Science News*, for example, recently included the item "Alcohol Answer? Drinks Lower Glucose to Protect Heart." This article postulates a mechanism by which ethanol protects the heart from disease. Any alcoholic drink, including wine, beer, or gin, lowers spikes in glucose levels after one eats a meal (without producing higher levels of insulin). Since high levels of blood glucose are known to be deleterious to heart health, moderate alcohol consumption helps to protect against type-2 diabetes and cardiovascular disease.[18]

The most important component in news like this is the word *moderate*. "While the results are a boon for people who drink moderately, Brand-Miller cautions that people shouldn't step up alcohol intake. Consuming more than one or two drinks daily would reverse the benefits."[19] These benefits accrue to people who are already drinking moderately and have not developed any tendencies toward addiction. No research article I have read advises people who do not currently drink to start drinking. It would be the pinnacle of irresponsibility to recommend a behavior that could possibly lead to the development of alcohol abuse, along with its destruction of health and even life. Clearly there are much better ways of dealing with type-2 diabetes than drinking alcohol in moderate quantities. Daily exercise, regulation of caloric intake

---

[17]Mayo Clinic Staff, "Red Wine and Resveratrol: Good for Your Heart?" available at http://www.mayoclinic.com/health/redwine/HB00089; accessed September 3, 2007.

[18]"Alcohol Answer? Drinks Lower Glucose to Protect Heart," *Science News* 171, no. 26 (June 30, 2007): 405.

[19]Ibid.

with attendant weight loss, avoidance of foods with high levels of refined carbohydrates, increased intake of whole grains and fiber, regular visits to a doctor, and use of appropriate medication are all superior to consuming alcohol in dealing with the problem of impaired glucose metabolism.

There have been so many articles on the benefits of drinking red wine that it is almost proverbial these days that moderate consumption is the ticket to cardiovascular health. These studies have stemmed from what has become known as the "French Paradox." French people love to eat foods that are rich in fat, loaded with cream and butter. Yet the French are noted for being lean and relatively free from heart disease. This seems paradoxical. Researchers have now postulated that a major contributing factor to this paradox is the consumption of moderate amounts of red wine, and the key compound may be the antioxidant resveratrol.[20]

Resveratrol (3,4,5-trihydroxystilbene) occurs naturally in grapes, red wine, purple grape juice, peanuts, and some berries (e.g., blueberries). Most of the studies to date have involved *in vitro* lab work, not controlled studies in humans. In the test tube resveratrol prevents the oxidation of low-density lipoprotein (LDL). It also could guard against cancer by preventing the formation of certain carcinogenic compounds. It further has been demonstrated to improve DNA repair in cells and activate pathways that lead to the death of possible cancer cells. Its one downside is the possible promotion of human breast-cancer cell development.[21]

Resveratrol is available as a nutritional supplement. Supplements allow for concentrations that are much higher than those found

---

[20]Melissa Q. B. McElderry, "Grape Expectations: The Resveratrol Story," available at http://quackwatch.com/01QuackeryRelatedTopics/DSH/resveratrol.html; accessed August 14, 2007.

[21]Ibid.

in a natural state. Unfortunately there have been no studies in humans that assess any of the resveratrol supplement's potential benefits. Human studies have shown that its bioavailability is low, a result of the body's rapid metabolism and elimination of the compound. It is unlikely that oral consumption of resveratrol supplements could produce blood plasma concentrations as high as those achieved during *in vitro* experiments.[22] Until more studies have been conducted, it is probably unwise for a person to begin consuming resveratrol supplements.

CONCLUSION

The Harvard School of Public Health, like all other reputable medical internet sites, maintains that there are proven health benefits of moderate alcohol consumption (one or two drinks per day for men, one for women) in fighting cardiovascular disease and in improving the body's ability to metabolize glucose. For younger adults, however, the risks of possible addiction outweigh any potential benefits. Women over 60 with a history of heart disease in their families might benefit from moderate alcohol intake, but they must realize that their chance of developing breast cancer would increase. Men over 60 who are at higher risk for heart disease might also benefit from one or two drinks per day. These benefits, however, come with a warning: "Given the complexity of alcohol's effects on the body and the complexity of the people who drink it, blanket recommendations about alcohol are out of the question."[23]

Because of the very real possibility of addiction and its associated physical and social ills, consuming alcohol for its medicinal benefit

---

[22]Jane Higdon, "Resveratrol," available at http://lpi.oregonstate.edu/infocenter/phytochemicals/resveratrol/; accessed August 14, 2007.

[23]Harvard School of Public Health, "Alcohol," available at http://www.hsph.harvard.edu/nutritionsource/alcohol.html; accessed August 14, 2007.

is neither necessary nor prudent.[24] Instead of drinking alcoholic beverages, there are vastly superior ways for people to increase their overall health and avoid cardiovascular disease. If someone is leading a sedentary lifestyle, the first step involves getting some sort of daily exercise. Perhaps the most accessible activity is simply walking. Good walking shoes are relatively inexpensive, and there are no expensive club memberships or equipment to purchase. Start with a slow walking pace for 30 minutes per day. Gradually increase the pace over the weeks, with the goal of covering two miles in 30 minutes. Remember that you do not have to train as if you were going to run a marathon in order to achieve significant health benefits.

Another key to heart health is proper nutrition. Decrease your consumption of refined carbohydrates (e.g., white bread, snack foods, and sugar) and start eating more whole grains, vegetables, and fruit. Select lean meats and other protein sources. Try to eat a couple of servings of fish per week, especially salmon or other species that are high in omega-3 fatty acid. If you can't avoid eating at fast-food restaurants, consult nutritional information that will facilitate wise choices. Above all, start cutting back on caloric intake by eating smaller portions. Most Americans are eating out more today than ever before. Because many restaurants are serving large portions, eat until you are satisfied, and take the remainder of your meal home in a take-out box. Good cardiovascular health ought to be the result of informed and determined lifestyle changes— not from the moderate consumption of alcoholic beverages.

---

[24]This is true even in the use of wine as an analgesic (cf. Prov. 31:6). Modern medicine offers painkillers that are far more effective and less risky than alcohol.

CHRISTLIKENESS AND DRINKING

Ultimately the choices we make in life do not stem from medical considerations alone, as important as they may be. Everything a Christian does must be the result of his desire to love and honor Christ. We have been called to a life of growing conformity to the image of Christ (Rom. 8:29), and that image involves holiness (Eph. 4:24; 1 Pet. 1:16–17). Growth in personal holiness ought to determine everything we are internally and everything we do externally.

PERSONAL HOLINESS HAS A POSITIVE FOCUS

Holiness is the word God has chosen in divine revelation to communicate the totality of His being. Out of all the definitions of holiness I've read, I like this one by A. S. Wood the best:

> Holiness is not merely one of God's attributes. It represents His essential nature. Holiness is His selfhood. When He swears by His holiness, He swears by Himself (Amos 4:2; 6:8; cf. Gen. 22:16; Pss. 89:35; 108:7). . . . It expresses His whole divine personality.[1]

Wood bases his definition on an interesting comparison of Amos 4:2 with 6:8. These two parallel verses declare that God takes an oath that judgment is coming on His people. Amos 4:2 says that the certainty of judgment is predicated on God's holiness. In parallel manner Amos 6:8 reveals that His *nephesh* ensures the sure fulfill-

---

[1]A. S. Wood, "Holiness," in *The Zondervan Pictorial Encyclopedia of the Bible*, ed. Merrill C. Tenney (Grand Rapids: Zondervan, 1976), 3:175.

ment of what He promises will happen. The Hebrew word *nephesh* refers to the totality of God's being. Taken together, the two verses indicate that God's holiness is the totality of His being. Logically, then, conformity to the image of Christ involves growth in holiness, the transformation of the believer's character into a finite reflection of the infinite aspects of God's being. We will never be divine, but God is working to turn conditions back to mankind's existence in the Garden of Eden before the fall of man into sin and death. Sanctification is foundationally a positive concept that entails becoming more like our Savior. As we read the Bible in search of what God has revealed about Himself, the Holy Spirit uses the Scripture to transform our character. This process of sanctification requires the believer to exercise diligence in the study of the Word, but the transformation of his character is entirely a work of supernatural grace.

Another positive aspect of sanctification is the believer's devotion to God and His will. In the Old Testament even inanimate objects are described as holy in this sense of being devoted entirely for God's use. Consider, for example, the holy status of all the wealth in the city of Jericho. Joshua carefully instructed his fellow Israelites that everything in the city was devoted[2] to the Lord. Consequently no Israelite was to keep any wealth for himself: "All the silver, and gold, and vessels of brass and iron, are consecrated unto the Lord: they shall come into the treasury of the Lord" (Josh. 6:19). The word translated "consecrated" is the Hebrew noun for *holiness*. The verse literally says, "All the silver, and gold, and vessels of brass and iron, are holiness to Yahweh." This passage teaches that the term for something that has been devoted exclusively for the Lord's use is synonymous with what is holy. Unfortunately

---

[2]The Hebrew word is חֵרֶם (*herem*), translated by the KJV as "accursed" or "accursed thing." The idea is something devoted to the Lord for whatever He purposes, whether total annihilation or exclusive use. See Leon J. Wood, "חָרַם," in *Theological Wordbook of the Old Testament*, ed. R. Laird Harris (Chicago: Moody Press, 1980), 1:324–25.

Achan was not listening carefully enough to Joshua's instructions. He saw some clothing, silver, and gold and took the items for his own use. His choice proved fatal (7:19–26). When the Lord determines that something is devoted to His use exclusively, He does not tolerate the abrogation of His will.

Throughout the Old Testament God declares that He has chosen Israel to be holy in this sense of being completely devoted to loving and obeying Him. Right after obtaining their freedom from Egyptian enslavement, for example, the Israelites came to Mt. Sinai and received this declaration from the Lord: "If ye will obey my voice indeed, and keep my covenant, then ye shall be a peculiar treasure unto me above all people: for all the earth is mine: And ye shall be unto me a kingdom of priests, and an holy nation" (Exod. 19:5–6). The word translated "peculiar treasure" (Heb. *segullah*) refers not to something odd or unusual but to what is most highly treasured.[3] Israel had an almost unbelievably privileged position, but the nation never experienced the full blessings of this status because the people were unfaithful to the stipulations of the promise. In fact Israel did not obey God's voice and refused to obey His covenant. They were not a holy nation because they turned from devotion to God.

God has commissioned the Church to experience what Israel failed to enjoy. In a wonderful example of the continuity between the Old and New Testaments, Peter makes it clear that we must fulfill what Israel never did:

> But ye are a chosen generation, a royal priesthood, *an holy nation*, a peculiar people; that ye should show forth the

---

[3]E. Lipinski notes that the term "implies both Yahweh's initiative and his personal engagement. This kind of acquired possession is valued more highly, and the word ultimately becomes the designation for any possession that one especially values." "סְגֻלָּה," in *Theological Dictionary of the Old Testament*, ed. G. Johannes Botterweck, Helmer Ringgren, and Heinz-Josef Fabry, trans. Douglas W. Stott (Grand Rapids: Eerdmans, 1990), 10:148.

praises of him who hath called you out of darkness into his marvelous light: which in time past were not a people, but are now the people of God: which had not obtained mercy, but now have obtained mercy. (1 Pet. 2:9–10, emphasis added)

Our transformed lives of devotion to Christ must be a continual display of God's holiness to unsaved people around us.

PERSONAL HOLINESS MANDATES A NEGATIVE RESPONSE TO THE WORLD SYSTEM

When Christians who are growing in holiness encounter the world system, the concept of holiness takes on a negative quality. Notice what Peter commands us immediately after describing the church as holy: "Dearly beloved, I beseech you as strangers and pilgrims, abstain from fleshly lusts, which war against the soul" (1 Pet. 2:11).

We must be sure we understand the difference between the *world* as the sum of all persons living on planet earth and the *world* as a domain of human existence with a system of values that Satan has created to entice people into living outside the will of God.[4] The former meaning of *world* is evident in John 3:16, a well-known verse that declares, "For God so loved the world, that he gave his only begotten Son." John uses the latter meaning of the term when he writes,

Love not the world, neither the things that are in the world. If any man love the world, the love of the Father is not in him. For all that is in the world, the lust of the flesh, and the lust of the eyes, and the pride of life, is not of the Father, but is of the world. And the world passeth away, and

---

[4]Joachim Guhrt describes the *world* in John's writings as "a uniform subject which opposes God in enmity, resists the redeeming work of the Son, does not believe in him, and indeed hates him (7:7; 15:18ff.). It is ruled by the prince of this cosmos (12:31; 16:11), i.e., the Evil One (1 John 5:18)." "κόσμος," in *The New International Dictionary of New Testament Theology*, ed. Colin Brown (Grand Rapids: Zondervan, 1975), 1:525.

the lust thereof: but he that doeth the will of God abideth forever. (1 John 2:15–17)

These three categories of strong enticement—fleshly, visual, and prideful—were exactly what Satan used in tempting both Eve (Gen. 3:6) and our Savior (Matt. 4:1–11).

Worldliness is a term that describes "an attitude of friendship toward, a desire for, and a wish to be recognized by the world system."[5] Worldliness in a Christian's heart violates the command of 1 John 2:15–17. We have to be careful that we do not stereotype worldliness, because it is foundationally an attitude, not an action. Satan is quite creative in tailoring many different forms of worldliness, because people vary widely in their tastes, aspirations, and affections. A form of worldliness that does not appeal to me may ensnare someone else, but I should not congratulate myself that I have not fallen to worldliness simply by avoiding what does not appeal to me!

Satan has successfully used a desire for illegal drugs to snare some people with the promise of fleshly enjoyment. Smoking marijuana, snorting cocaine, or shooting heroin has become an addictive lifestyle for millions of people worldwide. Such a lifestyle reflects worldliness by a devotion to physical pleasure (the lust of the flesh) above stewardship of the physical body (a recognition of the body's holiness, or devotion to God). I have never been tempted to experiment with drugs. But I must not conclude that I have no problem with worldliness simply because I consider the use of illegal drugs disgusting. Satan knows that he can find some form of worldliness that does appeal to me. I have to be on my guard continually so that the Devil does not use some aspect of the world system to draw my heart's affection away from Christ and His will.

[5]Mark Sidwell, *The Dividing Line: Understanding and Applying Biblical Separation* (Greenville, SC: Bob Jones University Press, 1998), 29. This book is a succinct and accurate presentation of biblical separation.

Satan can ensnare us even by using our affection for something that is not intrinsically wrong. Consider the recreational activity of private aviation. Being the pilot-in-command of an airplane is really a lot of fun. It is also amazingly convenient to travel from one general aviation airport to another in one's own aircraft—no fixed schedule to meet, no long security lines to endure, and no endless delays due to airline incompetence. If one is flying to a small airport far from a commercial flight connection, the time spent in travel is far less. The only unfortunate aspect of this mode of travel is its expense. For some people who are very highly paid, flying in private airplanes is cost-effective. It is entirely possible for a Christian to enjoy this activity and not manifest worldliness.

But what about a believer who really cannot afford to fly? Perhaps his enjoyment of owning an airplane has left him with excessive debt that has gotten unmanageable. He may center on the enjoyment and prestige that flying affords him, even though he has no money left for giving to his local church or other worthy ministries. Perhaps the euphoria of soaring through the clouds has trumped the biblical obligation of being a good steward of financial resources. An activity that might be perfectly acceptable for some believers has become a worldly trap for this person. Worldliness can be exceedingly subtle, just like the author of the world system (Gen. 3:1).

IS DRINKING ALCOHOL A FORM OF WORLDLINESS?

It is necessary at this point in our discussion to consider whether the consumption of alcoholic beverages is intrinsically wrong (like the use of illegal drugs) or something that a Christian might be able to enjoy without being entrapped by worldliness (like flying his own airplane). Since the Bible does not condemn drinking alcoholic beverages in moderation, could a believer enjoy a glass of his favorite vintage in the privacy of his home and not be ensnared by worldliness? Could he drink wine with dinner at a friend's home? Could he enjoy a pitcher of beer while watching a football game with his friends at the local sports bar? Since "the earth is the Lord's, and the fulness thereof" (Ps. 24:1; 1 Cor. 10:26), why not enjoy a cold brew?[6] These are issues that every Christian needs to settle by wisely applying biblical principles.

Let's not be naïve about our adversary's strategy. Paul admonished the believers at Corinth to be careful "lest Satan should get an advantage of us; for we are not ignorant of his devices" (2 Cor. 2:11). Satan has established the consumption of alcoholic beverages in our culture as an essential aspect of unsaved culture. Sophisticated drinkers seek the experience of collecting and consuming only the very best wines, often expending hundreds or even thousands of dollars on one bottle of a superior vintage. Alcohol has become by far the most widely abused drug in America. For the experience of temporarily forgetting how meaningless and empty their lives are, millions risk their health, marriages, children, jobs, and even their own lives by drinking to excess. Drinking is an easy escape from reality. My four years of association with hard-drinking engineering colleagues in the paper industry convinced me that alcohol consumption was not a peripheral activity in their lives—it was central and essential. The people I knew drank to get drunk; only inebriation brought a few hours of relief from their misery or boredom. So the broad spectrum of those who drink, all the way from the sophisticated wine connoisseur to the undiscriminating bum in the gutter, is united by the desire to have some experience that satisfies human pride or lust. Why would a Christian want *any* association with such a lifestyle?

Drinking alcoholic beverages is also a means by which worldly people know who shares their worldview. There is camaraderie and

---

[6]The use of this passage as an argument for consumption of alcohol reminds me of the man who argued that since God told Adam to use "every green herb" (Gen. 1:30), we should use the joy brought by smoking marijuana in the praise of God.

acceptance around the shared experience of drinking. One time I was in a management meeting of employees from a major paper company and heard an executive assure the group that he would never trust anyone who would not get drunk with him! For this fellow, drinking was an experience that had become a bond of solidarity among those who were committed to worldly culture.

A student of mine recently described his deliverance from the lifestyle of drinking. He was working for a car dealership in Denver when he came to know the Lord. He asked the Lord to take away his desire for alcohol, and God answered his prayer by making even the smell of it repugnant to him. He had only one subsequent encounter with drinking:

> I had no desire to drink until the dealership had a charity golf tournament. At that tournament a few of the employees and participants ordered Bloody Mary's [sic], an alcoholic drink consisting of vodka and tomato juice. I did not see the harm in having one, so I too ordered the same drink. As I was consuming my beverage, a gentleman to whom I had professed my Christianity approached me and asked if I were drinking a Bloody Mary. After I answered affirmatively, he made a statement that struck conviction into my heart. He said, "I didn't know Christians drank." I looked at my drink, which I had only partially consumed, and threw it out, saying, "You are right, we don't drink." I asked his forgiveness as well as God's and will look back on that day realizing that even unsaved people know what is right and wrong before a holy God.

Only Christians are naïve enough to think that consuming alcoholic beverages is simply a matter of personal Christian conscience—one of those "gray areas" that the Bible really doesn't address.

We must realize that everything we do as believers demonstrates whether we are sojourners in this present evil age or those who are seeking to find fulfillment in what the world system has to offer. It is vitally important that unsaved people who are watching our lives see evidence of the holiness that marks the transformed character and actions of those who profess to know Jesus Christ.

We must also guard our testimony with other believers. I may not even know, for example, that someone in the church I attend used to be an alcoholic before he or she was saved. I would not want to defile my conscience by knowing I did something that encouraged a fellow Christian to fall back into addiction to alcohol. Paul addressed this issue of living in a way that would not cause a fellow believer to fall into sin. In the context of 1 Corinthians 8:10–13, Paul was dealing with the issue of whether or not a Christian should eat meat at the venue of an idol's temple. The overall principle he states is just as applicable to the issue of drinking alcohol: "Wherefore, if meat make my brother to offend, I will eat no flesh while the world standeth, lest I make my brother to offend" (v. 13). When Paul states the same principle in Romans 14:21, he also includes the practice of drinking wine: "It is good neither to eat flesh, nor to drink wine, nor anything whereby thy brother stumbleth, or is offended, or is made weak." A Christian should want his life to be an example of devotion to Christ, not a model of how to flirt with the world system. The effect of his actions on the spiritual health of his brother is a primary consideration.

The example a believer sets in the home is even more important than his testimony in the church or society at large. Children are highly impressionable, and what they see a parent do at home they are prone to take even further in their own lives. Our Savior asserted the importance of providing children with a good example: "And whoso shall receive one such little child in my name receiveth me. But whoso shall offend [i.e., cause to stumble into sin] one of these little ones which believe in me, it were better for him that a millstone were hanged about his neck, and that he were drowned in the depth of the sea" (Matt. 18:5–6). I cannot even begin to imagine the grief of heart a parent would experience by realizing that the example he or she had set by consuming alcoholic beverages in the home influenced a child to drink excessively later in life.

CONCLUSION

The beverage use of alcohol is incompatible with growth in personal holiness; it hinders progress in being conformed to the image of Christ. A believer who drinks moderately risks setting a disastrous example for fellow Christians and the children who grow up in his own home. What he does in moderation could influence another person to become a drunkard. It is true that the Bible does not condemn the moderate consumption of alcoholic beverages within an ancient cultural setting that mandated their use for safe hydration as a necessary part of life. But drinking today is not comparable to biblical times. Modern drinks are far more intoxicating.[7] We have plenty of non-alcoholic options for safe hydration.[8] We ought to be growing in holiness and not cozying up to the world system. Let's be careful to set the biblical standard correctly for the generations that follow us. "Whether therefore ye eat, or drink, or whatsoever ye do, do all to the glory of God" (1 Cor. 10:31).

---

[7]Robert H. Stein confirms our earlier observation that the wine in biblical times was routinely diluted with water. "Is New Testament 'Wine' the Same as Today's Wine?" in *Difficult Passages in the New Testament* (Grand Rapids: Baker, 1990), 233–38.

[8]Norman L. Geisler notes that "people in the United States have plenty of wholesome, nonaddictive beverages. The situation today is unlike biblical times when there were not many wholesome beverages." Geisler's article is an excellent defense of abstinence from alcoholic beverages. "A Christian Perspective on Wine-Drinking," *Bibliotheca Sacra* 139 (Jan.–Mar. 1982): 53.